ADVANCE PRAISE FOR
REAL HAPPINESS

"Wonderfully clear, remarkably accessible, warmhearted and wise.
All you need to transform your life!" —JACK KORNFIELD,
author of *A Path with Heart* and
After the Ecstasy, the Laundry

"I have been waiting for this book! People ask me all the time to
recommend a book that will introduce them to the practice of
meditation. And while there are many books written on the subject,
none have brought together the purpose, technique, inspiration,
and science in such an integrated, intelligent, and personal way.
I will be suggesting and giving this jewel of a book to everyone I
know who wants to bring steadiness, grace, peace, and happiness
into their life through the practice of meditation."
—ELIZABETH LESSER,
Cofounder of Omega Institute and author of
Broken Open: How Difficult Times Can Help Us Grow

"Simply put, this is an awesome book from a truly excellent teacher.
Students constantly ask for recommendations on good books to
start and maintain a regular practice, and it's startling how few
really complete "nuts and bolts" practice manuals there are. This
book—complete with the whys, hows, and FAQs of practice—is
perfect for really accessing the power of meditation. I'll be telling
many students about it." —ETHAN NICHTERN,
author of *One City: A Declaration of Interdependence*

"In *Real Happiness* Sharon Salzberg introduces us with a gentle
but firm hand to the meditation experience. To those who have
taken her courses (like me) this book contains all of the jewels of
Sharon's teachings plus more." —RAM DASS,
author of *Be Here Now*

"Based upon ancient, timeless contemplative tradition as well as modern neuroscientific research and experiential neuroDharma experiments, Salzberg's four-week program for developing insight meditation, mindfulness, and her specialty of loving-kindness clearly instructs and awakens us, leading step by step to the discovery of who we are, why we are here, and how to realize a more fulfilling life and more harmonious world. I heartily recommend this to anyone seeking self-realization and inner peace, well being and enlightenment." —LAMA SURYA DAS

"Drawing on more than 30 years of experience teaching meditation, and as a participant in many dialogues with scientists on meditation research, Sharon Salzberg covers all the basics of meditation in a simple, compelling, and highly readable way. People frequently ask me where they should begin if they are interested in learning more about meditation. Now I know where to send them: *Real Happiness* is the perfect beginning." —DR. RICHARD J. DAVIDSON,
William James and Vilas Research
Professor of Psychology and Psychiatry
Director, Center for Investigating Healthy Minds
University of Wisconsin–Madison

"Reading *Real Happiness,* I feel as if I have made a new friend, or been reunited with an old one. Sharon Salzberg brings meditation to life and, through her grace, shows us how we can come alive, as well. This is a masterful work: deep, warm and engaging. I want to give it to everyone I know." —MARK EPSTEIN, M.D.
author of *Thoughts Without a Thinker*
and *Going to Pieces Without Falling Apart*

"In a voice that is wise and witty, personal, contemporary, and engagingly friendly, Sharon Salzberg has written this wonderful book that will be accessible and encouraging to novice meditators as well as inspiring to committed practitioners."

—SYLVIA BOORSTEIN,
author of *Happiness Is an Inside Job*

"This book is a veritable treasure box of meditations. Lucid and wise, *Real Happiness* is rich with Sharon Salzberg's lifetime of teaching meditation to thousands of people. Her voice is filled with humor, kindness, and wisdom, and her meditation instructions are practical and accessible. This is one of the great books on why and how to meditate." —ROSHI JOAN HALIFAX, Founding Abbot, Upaya Zen Center

"*Real Happiness: The Power of Meditation* is a highly accessible primer for anyone interested in exploring and undertaking the practice of meditation. Sharon Salzberg writes with love and clarity to give readers a week by week approach to living with mindfulness and compassion, both important to navigating busy lives in a world in need of healing from the inside out." —JACQUELINE NOVOGRATZ, Founder and CEO of Acumen Fund, author of *The Blue Sweater: Bridging the Gap Between Rich and Poor in an Interconnected World*, speaker at TED conferences

"In *Real Happiness,* Sharon Salzberg brings her astounding grace, humor, and glitteringly prose to the very basics of insight meditation. Friendly, comprehensive, and deadly serious, Salzberg grounds this 28-day beginner course in the gifts that meditation has given her in tough life situations. Since every mind is a beginner's mind, Salzberg outlines a path wide enough for everyone from today's wounded veterans; to ADD school kids; to distractable (and irritable) stay-at-home parents and CEOs. Meditation, she writes, unveils the "bright vein of goodness" available to all of us, all the time." —ELIZA GRISWOLD, author of *The Tenth Parallel: Dispatches from the Fault Line Between Christianity and Islam*

Real Happiness

10TH ANNIVERSARY EDITION

~~~

Real Happiness

**A 28-day Programme to
Connect with the
Power of Meditation**

Sharon Salzberg

HAY HOUSE

Carlsbad, California • New York City
London • Sydney • New Delhi

Published in the United States of America by:
Workman Publishing Company, Inc., 225 Varick Street, New York, NY 10014-4381
www.workman.com

Published in the United Kingdom by:
Hay House UK Ltd, The Sixth Floor, Watson House,
54 Baker Street, London W1U 7BU
Tel: +44 (0)20 3927 7290; Fax: +44 (0)20 3927 7291; www.hayhouse.co.uk

Published in Australia by:
Hay House Australia Ltd, 18/36 Ralph St, Alexandria NSW 2015
Tel: (61) 2 9669 4299; Fax: (61) 2 9669 4144; www.hayhouse.com.au

Published in India by:
Hay House Publishers India, Muskaan Complex, Plot No.3, B-2,
Vasant Kunj, New Delhi 110 070
Tel: (91) 11 4176 1620; Fax: (91) 11 4176 1630; www.hayhouse.co.in

Text © Sharon Salzberg, 2011, 2019

The moral rights of the authors have been asserted.

The information given in this book should not be treated as a substitute for professional
medical advice; always consult a medical practitioner. Any use of information in this
book is at the reader's discretion and risk. Neither the authors nor the publisher can be
held responsible for any loss, claim or damage arising out of the use, or misuse, of the
suggestions made, the failure to take medical advice or for any material on third-party
websites.

A catalogue record for this book is available from the British Library.

Trade paperback ISBN: 978-1-78817-468-8
Ebook ISBN: 978-1-78817-147-2

Illustrations: Phil Conigliaro
Illustration (pages 43, 44, and 93): Judy Francis Zankel
Mandala art: Clare Goodwin

MIX
Paper from
responsible sources
FSC
www.fsc.org   FSC® C013056

Printed and bound in Great Britain by
TJ International Ltd, Padstow, Cornwall

*To my teachers, who have
deeply realized the power of meditation,
and have always believed that I
(and all of us) could too.*

ACKNOWLEDGMENTS

~~~~~

There are several people who supported the evolution of this book to whom I am very grateful. Amy Gross has always wanted a book like this and has long encouraged me to write one; Nancy Murray brought me to Workman and reminded me both of why I wanted to be a writer and came up with the approach that got me going; Suzie Bolotin kept the faith for a long time.

Rachel Mann collated research; Joan Oliver brought clarity out of the tangle of questions and answers I had recorded; Joy Harris has always guided me superbly, and Ambika Cooper offered help in a thousand different ways.

Judith Stone, whose work was invaluable, has been an essential part of this project, and Ruth Sullivan has been a wonderful and extremely patient editor.

For this new edition a team of people at Workman Publishing has been of invaluable support: Anna Cooperberg, Mary Ellen O'Neill, Moira Kerrigan, Diana Griffin, Kate Karol, Barbara Peragine, Orlando Adiao, and Jacqueline Raposo.

May this book bring benefit and happiness to many.

CONTENTS

~~~

The 🔊 *icon indicates that this meditation is also available for download online. Go to hayhouse.co.uk/download and enter the following Product ID and Download Code. Product ID: 7390 – Download Code: ebook*

WEEK TWO

Mindfulness and the Body
Letting Go of Burdens 81

WEEK THREE

Mindfulness and Emotions
Dealing with Thoughts and Feelings.......................... 112

THE FIVE OBSTACLES

Introduction

TO THE NEW EDITION

ALL OF US INSTINCTIVELY WANT TO BE HAPPY, but all too often, lasting happiness eludes us. We may cherish an exquisite afternoon, try a new recipe to great success, or dare to imagine a better day, but a steady feeling of self-worth, inner strength, and genuine connection may seem unattainable. This inner struggle is what inspired me to write this book ten years ago. No matter what our particular circumstance, a daily mindfulness meditation practice can help us recognize the potential for true happiness that is within our grasp. In my more than four decades teaching, I have witnessed again and again how meditation transforms lives. It reduces our stress, focuses us, grounds us, connects us to ourselves, and gives us a sense of purpose. I wrote this book in the hope that it would make this route to happiness more widely known, more easily accessible, and more clearly understood.

Meditation was my path out of fragmentation and emotional pain. By the time I left for college at age sixteen, I'd lived in five different households. Each move was precipitated by the death of one of my family members or some kind of traumatic event. My family, like many others, did not openly discuss conflicts or loss. I felt alone and didn't know how I could be happy in life, but deep within me I believed it was possible.

In college in Buffalo, New York, I took an Asian philosophy course, which introduced me to meditation and the idea that a daily practice could train one's attention to be more focused, complete, open, and compassionate. Learning to be more present, better connected, and kinder to myself and others immediately suggested the prospect of greater happiness to me. The possibility of not just studying about meditation in the abstract, but actually experimenting with it and putting it into practice drew me like a magnet. I created a project and proposed that I go to India to study meditation. The university's independent studies program approved the proposal, and I arrived in India in the fall of 1970.

My focus was not the philosophy of meditative systems. I was seeking direct guidance on how to practice meditation to understand what benefits it might bring. One of the first things I discovered was that meditation wasn't as exotic or mystical as I'd expected—no magical set of instructions delivered in a darkened chamber with a supernatural aura. Instead, my teacher launched my practice with the words "Sit comfortably and feel your breath." *Feel my breath? I thought in protest. I could have stayed in Buffalo to feel my breath!*

I soon found out just how life-changing it was simply to focus my attention on inhaling and exhaling, and how that repeated action allowed me to be more in tune with myself. Building on awareness of the breath, I became more in touch with my body, with my emotions, with my thoughts, and with my intentions.

Over time, I learned how to place my punishing self-judgments in the broader context of the fullness of my life. I saw how every moment contains so many shades of meaning. I understood that learning to slow down, to attend to each breath as it arises and passes—and ultimately to attend to each moment and each encounter in the same way—establishes a sustainable form of happiness that naturally springs from living an authentic life.

Through meditation I found the bright vein of goodness that existed as a constant potential within me. As I grew to trust it, I saw that potential more clearly in the world around me. I realized that this ever-present potential was where true happiness resided.

The techniques themselves are timeless, but the broader manifestation of their use is ever growing. A 2018 survey by the National Center for Health Statistics showed that from 2012 to 2017, the use of meditation among American adults increased more than threefold, from 4.1% to 14.2%. This is an undeniable jump in meditators, showing that the results of meditation speak for themselves. It improves overall wellness; reduces stress, anxiety, pain, depression, or insomnia; and helps one deal with the emotional strain of chronic illness such as heart disease and cancer.

At the Insight Meditation Society in Barre, Massachusetts (which I cofounded in 1975), and around the world, I've taught the techniques you're about to encounter to—amongst others—Silicon Valley entrepreneurs, schoolteachers, police officers, teenagers, artists, Army chaplains and medics, doctors, nurses, burn patients, frontline workers in domestic violence shelters, international humanitarian aid workers, new empty-nesters, and new moms and dads.

Some meditation students, like me, seek a way to ease their stress and personal unhappiness. I've taught meditation to Patrick, a first responder to the 9/11 World Trade Center collapse, and (via email) to Dan, an Army reservist on active duty in Iraq. I've taught Stacey, a nurse who was just on the verge of burning out from the overwhelming expectations (her own and others) about her work, and Jo, who hasn't had a good night's sleep in a long while.

Some turn to meditation because they no longer want an unexamined existence of just living mechanically day after day. They know a deeper sense of purpose can come from looking at their habits and expectations, noticing what causes regret down the line, and seeing for themselves what brings them joy.

Lisa, the owner of small catering company, articulated what many I've taught hope to change about their lives. She said she "wanted to stop living in a fog. I'm on automatic pilot, disconnected from myself. I feel as if I'm living my life behind my own back." Through a more vibrant relationship to their experience, many find, it is possible to be happy even when life is not going seamlessly as planned, or when relationships or careers are more volatile than hoped for.

Beneath these varied motivations lies the essential truth that we're all alike in our vulnerability to pain and to the uncertainties of change, and all alike in wanting to discover and experience real happiness. Again and again I've seen novice meditators transform their lives—even if they came to the practice skeptical, antsy, belligerent, overconfident, or resistant. As I've learned through my own experience, meditation helps us to defuse stress, find greater tranquility, connect to our feelings, find a sense of wholeness, strengthen our relationships, and skillfully face our fears.

As I have gone around the world teaching the techniques in this book, I have seen that often the happiness we imagine is glittering and glamorous, that it means everything is going our way and that we're gliding through life grinning. We do have those moments, but when they come along, we hold on to them tightly, fearing that we may never feel something that special again. That kind of happiness is momentary, and it is not the particular happiness I'm inviting you to experience.

In one of the early interviews I did when the first edition of the book came out, a journalist asked if saying that the kind of happiness he experienced when he had a nice dinner with his wife was not real. I responded that I was not at all discounting what he felt in that lovely meal. Pleasure is wonderful when it comes our way, and I encourage everyone to savor joyful times. "If anything," I added, "if we were less distracted and more present, we would enjoy the evening even more." Yet what I believe is possible for us all is a quality of inner happiness that we could feel on a night when we don't like our dinner (or frankly, even our companion) all that much.

By knowing yourself better, being kinder to yourself and others, and having a better facility of connecting in the moment, you'll find that a deeper kind of happiness is available to you than just what is forthcoming at a tasty meal. It's a lasting tranquility, a sense of peace, a feeling of satisfaction.

The skills of meditation that will take you there are offered here in a simple week-by-week schedule. I offer an honest recounting of both the joys and challenges that we all face in meditation, so you need not ever feel you are all alone in this pursuit.

It is my hope that you will progress on your path to a richer and more sustained happiness by beginning or continuing your own meditation journey through the pages of this book.

CHAPTER I

What Is Meditation?

(OR, IF YOU CAN BREATHE, YOU CAN MEDITATE)

STRAIGHTFORWARD AND SIMPLE (but not easy), meditation is essentially training our attention so that we can be more aware—not only of our own inner workings but also of what's happening around us in the here and now. Once we see clearly what's going on in the moment, we can then choose whether and how to act on what we're seeing.

For the next four weeks, we'll be exploring the principles of insight meditation, the simple and direct practice of moment-to-moment awareness. We first train our attention by focusing on a single chosen object (most often our breath) and repeatedly letting go of distractions in order to return our attention to that object. Later we broaden the focus to include whatever thoughts, feelings, or sensations arise in the moment.

People have been transforming their minds through meditation for thousands of years. Every major world religion includes some form of contemplative exercise, though today meditation is often practiced apart from any belief system. Depending on the type, meditation may be done in silence and stillness, by using voice and sound, or by engaging the body in movement. All forms emphasize the training of attention.

ATTENTION, ATTENTION, ATTENTION!

"My experience is what I agree to attend to," the pioneering psychologist William James wrote at the turn of the twentieth century. "Only those items I notice shape my mind." At its most basic level, attention—what we allow ourselves to notice—literally determines how we experience and navigate the world. The ability to summon and sustain attention is what allows us to job hunt, juggle, learn math, make pancakes, aim a cue and pocket the eight ball, protect our kids, and perform surgery. It lets us be discerning in our dealings with the world, responsive in our intimate relationships, and honest when we examine our own feelings and motives. Attention determines our degree of intimacy with our ordinary experiences and contours our entire sense of connection to life.

The content and quality of our lives depend on our level of awareness—a fact we are often not aware of. You may have heard the old story, usually attributed to a Native American elder, meant to illuminate the power of attention. A grandfather (occasionally it's a grandmother) imparting a life lesson to his grandson tells him, "I have two wolves fighting in my heart. One wolf is vengeful, fearful, envious, resentful, deceitful. The other wolf is loving, compassionate, generous, truthful, and serene." The grandson asks which wolf will win the fight. The grandfather answers, "The one I feed."

But that's only part of the picture. True, whatever gets our attention flourishes, so if we lavish attention on the negative and inconsequential, they can overwhelm the positive and the meaningful. But if we do the opposite, refusing to deal with or acknowledge what's difficult and painful, pretending it doesn't exist, then our world is out of whack. Whatever doesn't get our attention withers—or retreats below conscious awareness, where it may still affect our lives. In a perverse way, ignoring the painful and the difficult is just another way of feeding the wolf. Meditation teaches us to open our attention to all of human experience and all parts of ourselves.

I'm sure you know the feeling of having your attention fractured by job and family, the enticement of electronic diversions, or the chatter of your mind—that morning's spat with your mate replaying in your head, a litany of worries about the future or regrets about the past, a nervous endless-loop recitation of the day's to-do list. Parts of that mental soundtrack may be old tapes that were instilled in childhood and have been playing so long we've nearly tuned them out of conscious awareness. These might be unkind pronouncements about the kind of person we are or preconceptions and assumptions about how the world works (for example: *Good girls don't act like that, men/women can't be trusted, you've got to look out for number one*).

We may no longer even notice the messages we're sending ourselves, just the anxiety that lingers in their wake. These habitual responses are often the result of a lifetime's conditioning—the earliest lessons from our parents and our culture, both explicit teaching and nonverbal cues.

This diffusion of attention can be mildly discomfiting, creating a vague sense of being uncentered or never quite there. It can be disheartening, leaving you exhausted from being dragged around by your jumpy, scattered thoughts; it can be downright dangerous (think of what can happen to distracted drivers). We can be lethally asleep at the wheel in other ways, too, neglecting relationships or failing to notice and act on what's really important to us. We miss a great deal because our attention is distracted or because we're so sure that we already know what's going on that we don't even look for new, important information.

Meditation teaches us to focus and to pay clear attention to our experiences and responses as they arise, and to observe them without judging them. That allows us to detect harmful habits of mind that were previously invisible to us. For example, we may sometimes base our actions on unexamined ideas

(I don't deserve love, you just can't reason with people, I'm not capable of dealing with tough situations) that keep us stuck in unproductive patterns. Once we notice these reflexive responses and how they undermine our ability to pay attention to the present moment, then we can make better, more informed choices. And we can respond to others more compassionately and authentically, in a more creative way.

HOW MEDITATION TRAINS ATTENTION: THE THREE KEY SKILLS

A ll forms of meditation strengthen and direct our attention through the cultivation of three key skills—concentration, mindfulness, and compassion or lovingkindness.

Concentration steadies and focuses our attention so that we can let go of distractions. Distractions waste our energy; concentration restores it to us. The introductory meditation technique you'll learn is uncomplicated and yet powerful: You'll improve your concentration by focusing on something you've known how to do all your life—breathing. The practice entails paying attention to each in-and-out breath, and when your mind wanders (it will, that's natural), noticing whatever has captured your attention, then letting go of the thought or feeling without berating yourself for it. You then return to focusing on your breathing. In this way meditation trains us to stay in the moment before us instead of reliving the past or worrying about the future. And it teaches us how to be gentle with ourselves and others, to forgive our lapses and move on. You'll learn more about concentration in Week One.

Mindfulness refines our attention so that we can connect fully and directly with whatever life brings. Mindfulness meditation moves our focus from a single object, the breath, to anything that's happening inside or outside of us at a given moment. We practice observing thoughts, feelings, sights, smells, sounds, without clinging to what's pleasant, pushing away what's painful, or ignoring what's neutral. And we become adept at catching ourselves in the act of substituting our habitual knee-jerk responses for a more accurate assessment of what's really going on in the present.

What might such a knee-jerk response look and feel like? Suppose, for instance, that someone says something that really riles us, and we feel a surge of anger. Maybe our automatic reaction to anger is to lash out before thinking at all. Or we might have a habit of judging *(if I feel anger, it means I'm a bad person)* that makes us deny the emotion churning inside; unexamined, it festers or grows in power. Or perhaps we're in the habit of projecting every emotion into an eternally unchanging future: *I'm an angry person, and I'll always be an angry person; I'm doomed!* None of these responses is likely to yield a happy outcome.

But if we apply mindfulness to the experience of anger, we can safely draw close to the emotion instead of fleeing, and investigate it instead of stonewalling. We notice it without judging it. We can gather more information about what happens when we get mad—what sets off the anger, where it lodges in the body, and what else it also contains, like sadness, fear, or regret.

This pause for nonjudgmental acknowledgment creates a bit of peaceful space within which we can make new, different choices about how to respond to something like anger. In this way we break old habits. We might decide to have a calm conversation with the person who's annoyed us instead of stewing or spewing; we might choose to leave the room until we cool down; or we might spend a few moments focusing on our breath in order to restore balance and perspective. Later, after our meditation session, we can think about the situations that tend to trigger our anger.

Mindfulness helps us get better at seeing the difference between what's happening and the stories we tell ourselves about what's happening, stories that get in the way of direct experience. Often such stories treat a fleeting state of mind as if it were our entire and permanent self. One of my favorite examples of this kind of globalizing came from a student who'd had an intensely stressful day. When she went to the gym later and was changing in the locker room, she tore a hole in her panty hose. Frustrated, she said to a stranger standing nearby, "I need a new life!"

"No you don't," the other woman replied. "You need a new pair of panty hose."

You'll learn more about mindfulness in Weeks Two and Three. In Week Two, we'll look at mindfulness and the body, and in Week Three, we'll work on dealing mindfully with our emotions.

continued on page 16

WHAT MEDITATION ISN'T

Many people have misconceptions about what meditation means. Before we begin, let me clear up a few of them.

It isn't a religion. You don't have to be a Buddhist or Hindu; you can meditate and still practice your own religion or no religion at all. Ben, the soldier who meditated while he was serving in Iraq, told me he thought the practice would help him stay in touch with his Christian values. The techniques you'll learn in this book can be done within any faith tradition. They can also be done in an entirely secular way.

It doesn't require special skills or background. Meditation isn't only for certain talented or already serene people. You don't have to be an ace at sitting still; you don't have to wait until you're uncrazed and decaffeinated. You don't need to study anything before you begin. You can start right now. If you can breathe, you can meditate.

It doesn't demand a huge chunk of your time every day. We're going to aim for twenty-minute sessions. If you like, you can start with five minutes and work your way up. (You'll find a more detailed discussion of the number and timing of meditation sessions on page 47 and in the "Nuts and Bolts" section of each chapter.) You'll probably want to lengthen your practice sessions, because you're going to like the sense of well-being they generate. But you don't have to. Establishing a *regular* practice, whatever the length of the session, is more important than striving to devote hours to it each day.

It doesn't eliminate sadness or rough patches from your life.
You're still going to have ups and downs, happiness and sadness.
But you'll be able to roll with the punches more and feel less
defeated, because meditation teaches us new ways of coping with
difficulties.

**It isn't an attempt to stop thinking or insist on only positive
thoughts.** That's not humanly possible. Meditation is a way to
recognize our thoughts, to observe and understand them, and
to relate to them more skillfully. (I like the Buddhist tradition of
replacing the modifiers "good" and "bad" to describe human
behavior with "skillful" and "unskillful." Unskillful actions are those
that lead to pain and suffering; skillful actions are those that lead to
insight and balance.)

**You don't have to renounce your opinions, goals, or passions;
you don't have to shun fun.** "If I start meditating," a woman
once asked me, "do I have to give up wanting things?" "No," I
told her. "You just have to relate differently to the wanting—pay
attention to it, investigate it, understand what's behind it." Adding
meditation to our lives doesn't mean withdrawing from the real
world of relationships, responsibilities, careers, politics, hobbies,
celebrations. In fact, it frees us to be more engaged with the things
that interest us, often in a healthier way.

It's not navel gazing. Meditation isn't self-indulgent or self-centered.
Yes, you'll learn about yourself—but it's knowledge that will help
you better understand and connect with people in your life. Tuning
in to yourself is the first step toward tuning in to others.

continued from page 13

Lovingkindness is compassionate awareness that opens our attention and makes it more inclusive. It transforms the way we treat ourselves, our family, and our friends. Spending time paying careful attention to our thoughts, feelings, and actions (positive and negative) and understanding them opens our hearts to loving ourselves genuinely for who we are, with all our imperfections. And that's the gateway to loving others. We're better able to see people clearly and to appreciate them in all their complexity if we've learned to care for and appreciate ourselves. We might then be more inclined to wish them well instead of becoming irritated, to let go of past hurts and deepen a connection to a relative—to offer a friendly gesture to someone we might previously have ignored, or find a better way to deal with a difficult person. In Week Four you'll learn specific techniques for increasing your compassion toward yourself and others.

During the 28-day program you're about to embark upon, you'll be systematically honing these skills. Each week's instruction will be divided into sections: the Practice Preview, which lets you know what to expect; the Meditations themselves; FAQs (real questions I hear again and again from my students); Reflections on the deeper lessons of the week; and the Takeaway, suggestions for incorporating the practice into everyday life.

Never have I seen a greater need for the gifts of meditation. Traveling the country, I constantly hear from the people I meet that they feel more and more fragmented by the demands and distractions of a complicated world, and anxious about its potential terrors. Meditation can give us a sense of wholeness and the security of a deep, confident calm that's self-generated.

People tell me they're saddened by the ugly, uncivil polarization they see in public life, and the isolation and loneliness they feel in private. They hunger for cooperation, connection, and community. Meditation, which teaches kindness, compassion, and patience, is a clear, straightforward method for improving relationships with family, friends, and everyone else we meet.

They tell me they're disheartened to discover that their accomplishments haven't increased their peace of mind and their possessions have brought only temporary satisfaction. Glory and gadgets have their place, but the only real app for happiness is a practice that creates a sense of ease within and can help us withstand sorrow and loss.

CHAPTER 2

Why Meditate?

THE BENEFITS AND
SCIENCE OF MEDITATION

I<small>F YOU'D LIKE TO GET STARTED</small> on your meditation program right away, you can turn to Week One (page 37). Or you can take a moment and learn more about the benefits of meditation in everyday life, and what scientists are discovering in the lab about the power of meditation, which is, in a nutshell, that meditation may be as important to your well-being as physical exercise.

Meditation is pragmatic, the psychological and emotional equivalent of a physical training program: If you exercise regularly, you get certain results—stronger muscles, denser bones, increased stamina. If you meditate regularly, you also get certain results. I've already mentioned some of them, including greater calm, and improved concentration and more connection to others. But there are other rewards. I'll discuss each of them at greater length in later chapters, and I'll explain how we get from here to there—from beginning to train our attention to living a transformed life.

You'll begin to spot the unexamined assumptions that get in the way of happiness. These assumptions we make about who we are and the way the world works—what we deserve, how much we can handle, where happiness is to be found, whether or not positive change is possible—all greatly influence how and to what we pay attention.

I was reminded of how assumptions can get in our way when I visited the National Portrait Gallery in Washington, D.C., to view a work of art by a sculptor friend. Eagerly I checked every room, peered at every display case and pedestal—no sculpture. Finally I gave up. As I headed for the exit, I glanced up—and there was her beautiful piece. It was a bas-relief hanging on the wall, not the free-standing statue I'd expected; my assumptions had put blinders on me and almost robbed me of the experience of seeing what was really there— her amazing work. In the same way, our assumptions keep us from appreciating what's right in front of us—a stranger who's a potential friend, a perceived adversary who might actually be a source of help. Assumptions block direct experience and prevent us from gathering information that could bring us comfort and relief, or information that, though saddening and painful, will allow us to make better decisions.

Here are some familiar assumptions you might recognize:

We have nothing in common.

I won't be able to do it.

You can't reason with a person like that.

Tomorrow will be exactly like today.

If I just try hard enough, I'll manage to control him/her/it/them.

Only big risks can make me feel alive.

I've blown it; I should just give up.

I know just what she's going to say, so I don't really need to listen to her.

Happiness is for other people, not me.

Statements like these are motivated by fear, desire, boredom, or ignorance. Assumptions bind us to the past, obscure the present, limit our sense of what's possible, and elbow out joy. Until we detect and examine our assumptions, they short-circuit our ability to observe objectively; we think we already know what's what.

You'll stop limiting yourself. When we practice meditation, we often begin to recognize a specific sort of conditioned response—previously undetected restrictions we've imposed on our lives. We spot the ways we sabotage our own growth and success because we've been conditioned to be content with meager results. Meditation allows us to see that these limits aren't inherent or immutable; they were learned and they can be unlearned—but not until we recognize them. (Some common limiting ideas: *She's the smart one, you're the pretty one. People like us don't stand a chance. Kids from this neighborhood don't* *become doctors.)* Training attention through meditation opens our eyes. Then we can assess these conditioned responses—and if parts of them contain some truth, we can see it clearly and put it to good use; if parts of them just don't hold up under scrutiny, we can let them go.

You'll weather hard times better. Meditation teaches us safe ways to open ourselves to the full range of experience—painful, pleasurable, and neutral—so we can learn how to be a friend to ourselves in good times and bad. During meditation sessions we practice being with difficult emotions and thoughts, even frightening or intense ones, in an open and accepting way, without adding self-criticism to something that already hurts. Especially in times of uncertainty or pain, meditation broadens our perspective and deepens our sense of courage and capacity for adventure. Here's how you get braver: little by little. In small, manageable, bearable increments, we make friends with the feelings that once terrified us. Then we can say to ourselves, *I've managed to sit down, face some of my most despairing thoughts and my most exuberantly hopeful ones without judging them. That took strength; what else can I tackle with that same strength?* Meditation lets us see that we can accomplish things we didn't think ourselves capable of.

You'll rediscover a deeper sense of what's really important to you. Once you look beneath distractions and conditioned reactions, you'll have a clearer view of your deepest, most enduring dreams, goals, and values.

You'll have a portable emergency resource. Meditation is the ultimate mobile device; you can use it anywhere, anytime, unobtrusively. You're likely to find yourself in situations—having a heated argument at work, say, or chauffering a crowd of rambunctious kids to a soccer game—when you can't blow off steam by walking around the block, hitting the gym, or taking a time-out in the tub. But you can always follow your breath. In Week One, you'll learn ways of practicing meditation wherever you are.

You'll be in closer touch with the best parts of yourself. Meditation practice cultivates qualities such as kindness, trust, and wisdom that you may think are missing from your makeup but are actually just undeveloped or obscured by stress and distractions. You'll have the chance to access these qualities more easily and frequently.

You'll recapture the energy you've been wasting trying to control the uncontrollable. I once led a retreat in California during a monsoonlike rainstorm. *It's so soggy and unpleasant that people aren't going to have a good retreat,* I thought. I felt badly for the participants; in fact, I felt responsible. For a few days I wanted to apologize to everybody for the rain until a thought flickered: *Wait a minute. I'm not even from California; I'm from Massachusetts. This isn't my weather. This is their weather. Maybe they should apologize to me!* And then the voice of deeper wisdom arose: *Weather is weather. This is what happens.*

We've all had weather moments—times when we've felt responsible for everyone's good time or well-being. It's our job, we think, to fix the temperature and humidity, or the people around us (if we could only get our partner to quit smoking, consult a map, stick to a diet!). We even think we're capable of totally controlling our own emotions—*I shouldn't ever feel envious, or resentful, or spiteful! That's awful! I'm going to stop.* You might as well say, "I'm never going to catch a cold again!" Though we can affect our physical and emotional experiences, we can't ultimately determine them; we can't decree what emotions will arise within us. But we can learn through meditation to change our responses to them. That way we're spared a trip down a path of suffering we've traveled many times before. Recognizing what we can't control (the feelings that arise within us; other people; the weather) helps us have healthier boundaries at work and at home—no more trying to reform everyone all the time. It helps us to stop beating up on ourselves for having perfectly human emotions. It frees energy we expend on trying to control the uncontrollable.

You'll understand how to relate to change better—to accept that it's inevitable and believe that it's possible. Most of us have a mixed, often paradoxical attitude toward change. Some of us don't think change is possible at all; we believe we're stuck forever doing things the way we've always done them. Some of us simultaneously hope for change and fear it. We want to believe that change is possible, because that means that our lives can get better. But we also have trouble accepting change, because we want to hold on permanently to what's pleasurable and positive. We'd like difficulties to be fleeting and comfort to stick around.

Trying to avoid change is exhausting and stressful. Everything is impermanent: happiness, sorrow, a great meal, a powerful empire, what we're feeling, the people around us, ourselves. Meditation helps us comprehend this fact—perhaps *the* basic truth of human existence, and the one we humans are most likely to balk at or be oblivious to, especially when it comes to the biggest change of all: Mortality happens, whether we like it or not. We grow old and die. (In the ancient Indian epic the *Mahabharata*, a wise king is asked to name the most wondrous thing in the universe. "The most wondrous thing in the entire universe," he says, "is that all around us people are dying and we don't believe it will happen to us.") Meditation is a tool that helps us accept the fact that everything changes all the time.

You'll soon discover that meditating offers a chance to see change in microcosm. Following our breath while observing how thoughts continually ebb and flow can help us realize that all elements of our experience are in constant flux. During a meditation session, you'll find it's natural to go through many ups and downs, to encounter both new delights and newly awakened conflicts that have bubbled up from the unconscious mind. Sometimes you'll tap into a wellspring of peace. Other times you might feel waves of sleepiness, boredom, anxiety, anger, or sadness. Snatches of old songs may play in your head; long-buried memories can surface. You may feel wonderful or awful. Daily meditation will remind us that if we look closely at a painful emotion or difficult situation, it's bound to change; it's not as solid and unmanageable as it might have seemed. The fear we feel in the morning may be gone by the afternoon. Hopelessness may be replaced by a glimmer of optimism. Even while a challenging situation is unfolding, it is shifting from moment to moment, varied, alive. What happens during meditation shows us that we're not trapped, that we have options. Then, even if we're afraid, we can find a way to go on, to keep trying.

This is not a Pollyanna-ish sentiment that everything will be just fine, according to our wishes or our timetable. Rather it is an awakened understanding that gives us the courage to go into the unknown and the wisdom to remember that as long as we are alive, possibility is alive. We can't control what thoughts and emotions arise within us, nor can we control the universal truth that everything changes. But we can learn to step back and rest in the awareness of what's happening. That awareness can be our refuge.

And science has now proven that change is possible on a cellular level as well.

THE SCIENCE OF MEDITATION

When I was in high school, we were taught as irrefutable truth that the size and circuitry of the brain are fixed before adulthood. But in the last decade and a half, neuroscientists and psychologists have demonstrated again and again that the adult brain is capable of neuroplasticity— that is, forming new cells and pathways. Throughout life, the brain rewires and reshapes itself in response to environment, experience, and training. And meditation is one of those brain-changing experiences. A number of recent studies confirm that meditation can bring about significant physiological changes in the brain that create welcome changes in health, mood, and behavior.

Advances in brain monitoring and imaging have made it possible to watch the brain in action during meditation. The amazing news coming from researchers all over the world is that the practice of meditation seems to prime brain cells to fire together in patterns that strengthen key brain structures—those, for example, important in tasks such as decision-making, memory, and emotional flexibility. And it may also improve communication among different parts of the brain in ways that further improve physical and emotional health.

In 2005, a pioneering study led by neuroscientist Sara Lazar of Harvard University and Massachusetts General Hospital showed that practitioners of insight meditation had measurably thicker tissue in the left prefrontal cortex, an area of the brain important for cognitive and emotional processing and well-being. And the subjects of her study weren't Tibetan monks who'd spent years contemplating in caves, but ordinary Boston-area professionals, most of whom meditated about 40 minutes a day. Brain scans of the older participants suggest that meditation may also counteract the thinning of the cortex that occurs naturally with aging, and thus may protect against memory loss and cognitive deficits.

Several other brain-scan studies have extended Lazar's work, showing that meditation strengthens areas of the brain involved in memory, learning, and emotional flexibility. In 2009, for example, neuroscientist Eileen Luders of the

UCLA Laboratory of Neuro Imaging reported that when she and her team compared the brains of experienced practitioners of insight meditation with those of a control group of non-meditators, they found that the brains of the meditators contained more gray matter—the brain tissue responsible for high-level information processing—than did those of the non-meditators, especially in the areas of the brain associated with attention, body awareness, and the ability to modulate emotional responses. "We know that people who consistently meditate have a singular ability to cultivate positive emotions, retain emotional stability, and engage in mindful behavior," says Luders. "The observed differences in brain anatomy might give us a clue why meditators have these exceptional abilities."

And in a study published in 2010, Lazar and her team scanned the brains of volunteers before and after they received eight weeks of training in Mindfulness-Based Stress Reduction (MBSR), a popular combination of meditation and yoga designed to alleviate stress in patients with health problems. The new meditators showed measurable changes in two important brain areas—growth in the hippocampus, a part of the brain involved in memory and learning, and shrinkage in the amygdala, a portion of the brain that initiates the body's response to stress. The decrease in the size of the amygdala correlated with lowered stress levels reported by the group that learned meditation—and the more they reduced their stress through meditation, the smaller the amygdala got. A control group that received no MBSR training showed no such brain changes on scans done eight weeks apart.

A 2012 study published in *Frontiers of Human Neuroscience* supports this: It also gave volunteers with no prior meditation experience eight weeks of Mindful Attention Training, which is similar to MBSR. Then, using fMRI scans, the researchers found that amygdala activation *decreased* when the participants were presented with positive, neutral, and negative images. Because the scans were taken when the participant wasn't meditating, this further supports a growing body of research suggesting that meditators excel in present-moment awareness and are able to regulate emotions in response to stimuli of any kind. When we can regulate our emotions in the moment, we feel more emotionally stable overall.

More and more studies like these are finding measurable evidence of what meditators have known empirically for centuries: Meditation strengthens the brain circuits associated not only with concentration and problem solving, but with our feelings of well-being. In other words, science has shown that meditation just plain makes people happier.

"We now know that the brain is the one organ in our body built to change in response to experience and training," says Richard Davidson, Ph.D., an expert in the study of neuroplasticity. "It's a learning machine." A professor of psychology and psychiatry at the University of Wisconsin, Davidson is the founding director of the school's Center for Healthy Minds, launched in 2010 to further the new discipline of contemplative neuroscience, the study of how meditative practices affect brain function and structure and how those changes affect physical and emotional health.

What's most heartening about the new research, says Davidson, is the way meditation can remodel the brain to strengthen the qualities that psychologists say are crucial components of happiness: resilience, equanimity, calm, and a sense of compassionate connection to others. "We don't take this revolutionary idea as seriously as we should," says Davidson. "Emotions—and happiness in particular—should be thought of in the same way as a motor skill. They can be *trained.*" In one of Davidson's own experiments, which we include in Week Four, he found that lovingkindness meditation actually changes the way the brain works so that we become more compassionate (see page 186). "One thing all these studies show," says Harvard's Sara Lazar, "is that, as with physical exercise, the more you practice meditation, the greater the benefit. It's really clear that the more you do, the more you get."

Meditation has also been studied for how it affects our ability to have compassion for others. In 2013, a team of researchers at Northeastern University and Harvard Medical School tested the effects of meditation in circumstances that required compassionate decision-making. After being led in eight weeks of meditation practice, participants were called to the lab under the guise of taking cognitive tests and told to sit in the waiting room. The waiting room was the test: two of three chairs in the space were filled by confederates in on the study, leaving one chair for the participant. Eventually, a third confederate came into the room with crutches and a walking boot. Meditation played a large part in triggering a compassionate response, as meditating participants offered their seat to the sufferer five times more often than those in the control group who did not participate in meditation training.

A 2018 study led by Kathryn Adair at Duke University and Barbara Fredrickson at The University of North Carolina at Chapel Hill tested the theory that mindfulness would increase feelings of social connection. Participants took part in a six week mindfulness meditation course or in a control course, and were assessed for their levels of social connection, decentering (that is, stepping back and being aware of one's thoughts and actions rather than acting and reacting), and general emotions pre- and post- training. After six weeks, the meditators were able to achieve a mindful outlook even while not performing mindfulness exercises and reported that this gave them a sense of greater social connection—which predicts greater positive emotions overall.

Scientists have also looked at the way meditation improves attention. In a 2019 fMRI study, researchers at the Center for Healthy Minds aimed to show that mindfulness training improves the connection between two networks in the brain that are integral to attentional control and focus. In the study, participants were randomly assigned to one of three groups: one that received Mindfulness-Based Stress Reduction (MBSR) training, one that received training similar to MBSR that didn't have a mindfulness component, and a control group that was placed on a "waitlist" and received no training. All had an fMRI brain scan before and after eight weeks, and again five to six months after the study ended.

The researchers found that, for the first group, the connection between the two brain networks strengthened after eight weeks compared to the other groups, and held steady at the final scan five to six months later.

In 2007, researchers at the University of Pennsylvania trained a group of non-meditators in MBSR, then compared this group both with longtime meditators taking part in a month-long meditation retreat and with a control group who had no experience with meditation. After eight weeks of training, the new meditators improved their scores for orienting, or turning one's attention to a specific thing, and for sustaining attention. The veteran meditators showed greater skill at conflict-monitoring—choosing what to focus on among competing stimuli—than did either of the other two groups, and they were better able to filter distracting stimuli in order to remain focused. These findings suggest that meditation may be useful for improving cognition and other attention-based functions that slow as we age.

Since then, many studies have been conducted to explore how mindfulness practices affect those with ADHD. More research is needed in the area, but the vast majority of trials do suggest that mindfulness could be a promising method for treating ADHD.

Training attention through meditation also improves our capacity to process rapidly arriving incoming information. When we're presented with two new pieces of visual information in very quick succession, we have trouble detecting the second stimulus because the brain's limited attentional resources are still busy processing the first one, a phenomenon called the "attentional blink." But the fact that we can detect the second stimulus at least some of the time shows that the attentional blink is subject to training. Curious about our ability to improve cognitive functioning, neurobiologist Heleen Slagter and colleagues at the University of Wisconsin recruited participants in a three-month meditation retreat and evaluated their attentional blink rates before and after. They found that newly trained meditators were able to reduce the attentional blink substantially by the end of the retreat. The study supports the idea that attention can be trained and improved.

Perhaps this is one reason meditation seems to work so well for athletes. Famed basketball coach Phil Jackson, a meditator himself, arranged to have his players—first the Chicago Bulls and then the L.A. Lakers—learn meditation as a way to improve their focus and teamwork. Jackson finds that mindfulness assists players in paying attention to what's happening on the court moment by moment. Such precise training in attention has paid off during tense playoffs: Jackson has led more teams to championships than any coach in NBA history.

Meditation seems to improve not just our cognitive abilities, but also our immune system. In one study, for example, Davidson and colleagues teamed with Jon Kabat-Zinn, Ph.D., founder of the Stress Reduction Clinic at the University of Massachusetts Medical Center and the developer of MBSR. The scientists studied the brains of participants before and after they received eight weeks of MBSR training and compared them with those of a group of nonmeditators. At the end of the training, the subjects received flu shots and their antibody activity was tested. Not only did the meditators show elevated activity in the area of the brain associated with lowered anxiety, a decrease in negative emotions, and an increase in positive ones, but their immune systems produced more antibodies in response to the vaccine than did the nonmeditators'. In other words, there may be a strong link among meditation, positive emotions, and a healthier immune system.

Because of these studies, some doctors are recommending meditation to patients with chronic pain, insomnia, and immune deficiencies. Clinicians regularly use mindfulness meditation as part of therapy, especially with clients who have anxiety, depression, or obsessive-compulsive disorders. Therapists have come to realize that meditation may alter reactions to daily experience at a level that words cannot reach. "It's a shift from having our mental health defined by the content of our thoughts," says psychologist Steven Hayes of the University of Nevada, "to having it defined by our relationship to that content—and changing that relationship by sitting with, noticing, and becoming disentangled from our definition of ourselves."

Among the institutions that have embraced meditation as a legitimate area of scientific study is the U.S. government. Over the years, the National Institutes of Health's National Center for Complementary and Integrative Health (NCCIH) has greatly increased the number of meditation studies it sponsors. Current projects include looking into how mindfulness can help law enforcement officers manage stress, the effect of mindfulness on migraine pain, how a lovingkindness practice makes a difference in decision-making, and the effect compassion training has on veterans with PTSD.

A 2019 study led by Amishi Jha at the University of Miami gave members of the military training in mindfulness for four weeks and found that, compared to those who were given only two weeks of training or no training at all, both their ability to be attentive during chaotic circumstances and their working memory improved. The participants also reported that they were making fewer cognitive errors than before. The effect of these ancient practices on performance cannot be denied.

For many people, science provides a way of understanding the world that allows them to approach subjects they might otherwise have dismissed. One of the most wonderful things about these findings, beyond the personal improvements they promise, is that a large, new group of people may now feel more comfortable about taking advantage of meditation's many benefits.

These benefits accrue not simply from reading about and admiring the effects of meditation, but from actually practicing it.

KICKING OPEN THE DOOR

A t Bob Dylan's induction into the Rock and Roll Hall of Fame in 1988, Bruce Springsteen described hearing Dylan's music for the very first time. Springsteen was fifteen, he said, riding in the car with his mother, idly listening to the radio, when "Like a Rolling Stone" came on. It was as though, Springsteen recalled, "somebody took his boot and kicked open the door to your mind." His mother's verdict: "That man can't sing." Mrs. Springsteen's response reminds us that we don't all react the same way to the same experience—and her son's reminds us that life holds moments when our perspective dramatically shifts, when our assumptions are deeply challenged, when we see new possibilities or sense for the first time that whatever has been holding us back from freedom or creativity or new ventures might actually be overcome.

There are moments when we sense that tomorrow doesn't have to look like today—that the feeling of defeat that's been flattening us for what seems like forever can lift, that our anxiety needn't define us, that the delight we've been postponing and the love we long for could be nearer at hand than we'd thought.

Sometimes a flash of inspiration kicks open that door: We hear a piece of music, see a work of art, read just the right poem. Or we meet someone who has a big vision of life, someone we admire who embodies values we cherish. Life seems to hold more possibilities.

Sometimes pain kicks open that door: We lose our job or lose a friend; feel betrayed or deeply misunderstood. In our distress, we suddenly feel an urgent need to look more deeply for understanding and an abiding sense of well-being.

If you're reading these words, perhaps it's because something has kicked open the door for you, and you're ready to embrace change. It isn't enough to appreciate change from afar, or only in the abstract, or as something that can happen to other people but not to you. We need to create change for ourselves, in a workable way, as part of our everyday lives. That's what the next four weeks of learning to meditate will do.

The door of possibility has been opened—the door to authentic and accessible happiness. Welcome. Come in and sit.

Concentration

BREATHING AND THE ART
OF STARTING OVER

I MAGINE RECLAIMING ALL THE ENERGY that could be available to us but isn't because we scatter it, squandering it on endlessly regretting the past, worrying about the future, berating ourselves, blaming others, checking Facebook yet again, throwing ourselves into serial snacking, workaholism, recreational shopping, recreational drugs.

Concentration is a steadying and focusing of attention that allows us to let go of distractions. When our attention is stabilized in this way energy is restored to us—and we feel restored to our lives. This week you're going to learn techniques for deepening concentration through focusing on the breath.

Sometimes distractions are internal—the continuous replaying of old mistakes and regrets *(Why didn't I listen to my dad?* or *If only I'd married Jeffrey)* or the nursing of past injustices *(How could she have accused me of disloyalty? I was the one who stuck up for her!).* We focus on things we can't undo. Or we throw our energy into obsessively fantasizing about a future that may never happen *(What if I tell the committee my ideas and they put me down? Or what if they steal my ideas, and don't give me credit? I'll quit!)* and then getting terribly agitated about it, as if the woes we're imagining had already come to pass. "I've been through some terrible things in my life, some of which actually happened," Mark Twain once said. Or we live in a state of perpetual postponement that blinds us to the potentially fulfilling moment in front of us: *I'll be happy when I graduate,* we tell ourselves, *when I lose ten pounds, when I get the car/the promotion/the proposal, when the kids move out.*

And plenty of the distractions are external: the familiar competing tugs of home and work; the twenty-four-hour media matrix; our noisy consumer culture. We often try to buy our way out of pain, regarding material possessions as talismans against change, against loss and death. "Getting and spending, we lay waste our powers," the poet William Wordsworth wrote.

And not just getting and spending; also texting, Web surfing, tweeting, Skyping, digitally recording. A colleague recently led stress-reduction sessions for people who felt themselves to be suffering from an excess of distraction, an inability to settle and simply be. One man complained that he didn't have enough time in the day, that he felt disconnected from his family and generally anxious. When my friend asked him how he typically spent his time, the man described reading an average of four newspapers and watching at least three TV news shows every day.

Relearning how to concentrate, says the writer Alain de Botton, is one of the great challenges of our time. "The past decade has seen an unparalleled assault on our capacity to fix our minds steadily on anything," he wrote in the 2010 essay "On Distraction." "To sit still and think, without succumbing to an anxious reach for a machine, has become almost impossible."

Linda Stone, a former executive at both Apple and Microsoft, has coined the term Continuous Partial Attention to describe a pervasive and exhausting condition you're likely to find familiar. Simple multitasking—it seems almost quaint—was, she says, motivated by the desire to be more productive and to create free time for friends, family, and fun. "But Continuous Partial Attention is motivated by a desire not to miss anything," she writes. "We're talking on the phone and driving; carrying on a conversation at dinner and texting under the table. . . . Continuous Partial Attention involves an artificial sense of constant crisis, of living in a 24/7, always-on world. It contributes to feeling stressed, overwhelmed, overstimulated, and unfulfilled; it compromises our ability to reflect, to make decisions, and to think creatively."

Not that there isn't a place for video games or shopping or watching the news avidly. It's moderation and conscious deployment we're after—knowing what we're doing when we're doing it, rather than being on automatic pilot and turning to these activities out of habit. The point is not to hate the stuff we've bought, or berate ourselves for being a news junkie, or withdraw from modern life, but to be willing to experiment with our time and attention, connecting more fully with our life as it happens. Concentration lets us put on the brakes and spend time just being with what is, rather than numbing out or spinning away into excess stimulation.

The larger effect of distraction is a disconcerting sense of fragmentation. We often feel uncentered; we don't have a cohesive sense of who we are. We find ourselves compartmentalizing, so that the person we are at work is different from the one we are at home. We might be confident in the office and fragile at home, or vice versa; withdrawn with our spouse but the life of the party when we're out with our friends. Our best self, the one who values patience and compassion, isn't the same self who snaps at the kids. Or as a student said to me recently, "I'm filled with lovingkindness and compassion for all beings everywhere—as long as I'm alone. Once I'm with someone else, it's really rough." For some of us, it's the other way around; we're fine when we're with others but ill at ease in our own company.

Each of us is, of course, a combination of many traits, states of mind, abilities, and drives; they're all part of us. Some qualities are paired opposites, and we can spend a lifetime resolving and integrating competing characteristics and needs—for both intimacy and independence, for vulnerability and strength. When our attention is tuned in, when we're aware of ourselves, these different parts of us work in concert and in balance; when we're distracted, they don't, and that's when we feel fragmented and compartmentalized. Meditation—training our attention—allows us to find an essential cohesiveness.

GETTING READY: SOME PRACTICAL PREPARATION

~~~~

CHOOSING A PLACE

Establish a meditation corner you can use every day. It could be in your bedroom or office; in the basement or on the porch. Wherever you practice, pick a place where you can be relatively undisturbed during your meditation sessions. Turn your cell phone, other mobile devices, and laptop off and leave them in another room.

Traditionally people sit on a cushion on the floor. If that doesn't work for you, you may sit in a straight-backed dining room or kitchen chair, or on the couch. (If you're unable to sit at all, you may lie down on your back with your arms at your sides.) If you're sitting on the floor, a pillow or sofa cushion is fine; you can also buy a special cushion meant especially for meditating, or a meditation bench that lets you sit in a supported kneeling position. (You'll find a list of sources for these items on page 217.) Some people decorate their meditation place with meaningful objects or images. Others bring an inspiring book from which they read a short passage before meditating.

WHAT TO WEAR

"Distrust any enterprise that requires new clothes," Henry David Thoreau said. He'd have been pleased to learn that meditation calls for no special outfit. Comfortable clothes are best. But if you find yourself stuck in uncomfortable ones, don't let that stop you.

CHOOSING A TIME

Plan to meditate at about the same time every day. Some people find it best to sit first thing in the morning; others find it easier to practice at lunchtime, or before going to bed at night. Experiment to find the time that works best for you. Then make a commitment to yourself. Write it in your datebook.

I suggest you start by sitting for twenty minutes of meditation three times the first week—but if you'd rather start with a shorter time and gradually lengthen it, that's fine. Decide before each session how long it's going to be. (Set an alarm if you're worried about knowing when the time is up.) The guided meditations in this book are between ten and twenty minutes long. You'll add one more day of meditation in Week Two, another in Week Three, and two in Week Four, so that by the end of the month you'll have established a daily practice.

Formalizing a time to meditate will enhance your sense that this is a deeply important activity. But here's the fundamental question: What will get you to sit down on that cushion or chair? Sometimes people think, *If I don't have an hour, I won't do it.* Even five minutes, though, if that's all you have, can help you reconnect with yourself.

POSTURE

Spend some time at the beginning of each session settling into the posture; the first thing you need to do is really inhabit your body. The traditional components of meditation posture have been used for many centuries. At first they may feel odd and uncomfortable, but you'll come to be at ease with them.

Legs: If you're on a cushion, cross your legs loosely in front of you at the ankles or just above. (If your legs fall asleep during meditation, switch and cross them the other way around, or add another cushion for a higher seat.) Your knees should be lower than your hips.

People who are unable to cross their legs can sit with one leg folded in front of the other without crossing them. You can also kneel by using a meditation bench or by placing a cushion behind you between your thighs and calves, as if you were sitting on a short bench. If you're sitting on a chair, keep your feet flat on the floor. That will help you sit up straight so your breathing can be more natural.

A simple meditation posture, with legs crossed easily.

Back: Whether you're on a cushion or a chair, the way you hold your back is the most important part of the meditation posture. Sit up straight, but don't strain or go rigid. Picture your vertebrae as a neat stack of coins. The natural curve at the small of your back will help support you.

Maintaining a straight spine helps you breathe more naturally and stay alert. If you're sitting in a chair, try not to lean against the back of it, in order to keep your spine straight. With your spine stacked this way, your hips are level, your shoulders are level, and you are a balanced, solid triangle.

Arms and hands: Let your hands fall naturally onto your thighs, resting palms down. Don't grab on to your knees, or use your arms to support the weight of your torso. Some meditators prefer to arrange their hands in this way: Cup your right hand in your left, palms up, with the tips of your thumbs barely touching and forming a triangle with your hands.

Some meditators prefer to rest their hands in this position.

Head: When you're seated with a straight spine, look levelly in front of you. This drops your head very slightly forward. When you lower your gaze or close your eyes (see below), maintain this position. Keep your shoulders relaxed; if you find them rising into a shrug, gently lower them.

Eyes: Close your eyes, but don't squeeze them shut. If you're more comfortable with your eyes open (or if you find yourself dozing off), gaze lightly at a point about six feet in front of you and slightly downward. Soften your eyes—don't let them glaze over, but don't stare hard, either.

Jaw: Relax your jaw and mouth, with your teeth slightly apart. A teacher once told me to part my lips just enough to admit a grain of rice.

PRACTICE PREVIEW

⁓

This week, you begin learning how to use concentration to overcome myriad distractions in your life.

You'll start on the most intimate and workable level: Week One's meditation sessions will be devoted to improving concentration by aiming your attention at your breath as it moves in and out of your body. We choose the breath as our focus because it's something we do naturally: There's no intentional effort involved. (If you have respiratory problems, or you've tried several times to follow the breath and found that doing so makes you anxious, experiment with focusing on sounds, as in the Hearing Meditation in this chapter, or use the Body Scan Meditation that you'll find in Week Two.)

Thoughts and feelings will inevitably arise and claim your attention, but you'll practice repeatedly noticing and letting go of these distractions, then returning your awareness to the *in* and *out* of your breath. Breathing, discovering you've been distracted, and starting over: simple and manageable.

Some of these thoughts and feelings may be fascinating and delightful; some may make you uncomfortable; some may be deadly dull. You'll practice letting them all go, without taking the time to judge them. This is a crucial first step in learning how to be more centered and present.

Almost immediately you'll feel the healing power of being able to begin again, no matter where your attention has gone or for how long. Everyone who meditates, beginners and longer-term practitioners alike, gets hijacked at times by thoughts and feelings; it's impossible not to be. But once you see how doable it is to start over, you won't judge your efforts so harshly. And you'll learn that starting over and not fruitlessly berating yourself are skills you can bring into your everyday life when you've made a mistake or lost sight of your aspirations. You can begin again.

Another healthy result of concentration: It brings wholeness when we feel scattered, because we allow ourselves to be aware of all of our feelings and thoughts, the pleasant and the painful ones. We don't have to exhaust ourselves by running away from difficult or troubling thoughts, or by keeping them hidden, or by beating ourselves up for having them. And because we've begun to be kinder to and more accepting of ourselves, we can be kinder to and more accepting of others.

As meditation moves us toward wholeness, we rediscover a strong center, an inner store of mental and emotional strength that was once lost to us. Many people who practice concentration to steady their attention use the same word to describe the feeling it gives them: empowered. Once we have a sense of a center, we can more easily withstand the onslaught of overstimulation, uncertainty, and anxiety the world launches at us without getting overwhelmed. We're stronger because we not only see more but also see more clearly. When your attention is diffuse, it's like a broad, weak beam of light that doesn't reveal much. Concentration brings the weak beam down to a single, sharply focused, supremely bright, exponentially more illuminating point.

You may not be convinced that sitting and breathing can lead to personal transformation. But you'll soon have the opportunity to test this for yourself; your meditation practice is about to begin. Don't worry about getting it right. When your mind wanders, as it inevitably will, don't be alarmed. Just notice whatever has captured your attention, then let go of the thought or feeling and gently bring your attention back to the breath. No matter how far away you drift, or for how long, don't be concerned. If you get tangled up in thoughts, release them and start over. If you feel bored, or panicked, start over. If you can't sit still, start over. If one day this week you just can't find the time or the will to meditate, start over the next day.

NUTS AND BOLTS

In Week One, try to do a twenty-minute sitting meditation on three days of this week. You can use the following Core Breathing Meditation or you can try one of the two variations offered in this chapter—the Hearing Meditation and the Letting-Go-of-Thought Meditation. You might also practice incorporating the mini-meditations suggested on page 58 into your day.

THE CORE MEDITATION:
BREATHING*

This classic meditation practice is designed to deepen concentration by teaching us to focus on the *in* and *out* breath.

Sit comfortably on a cushion or a chair in the posture detailed on pages 43–44. Keep your back erect, but without straining or overarching. (If you can't sit, lie on your back, on a yoga mat or folded blanket, with your arms at your sides.)

You don't have to feel self-conscious, as though you're about to do something special or weird. Just be at ease. Close your eyes, if you're comfortable with that. If not, gaze gently a few feet in front of you. Aim for a state of alert relaxation.

Deliberately take three or four deep breaths, feeling the air as it enters your nostrils, fills your chest and abdomen, and flows out again. Then let your breathing settle into its natural rhythm, without forcing or controlling it. Just feel the breath as it happens, without trying to change it or improve it. You're breathing anyway. All you have to do is feel it.

Notice where you feel your breath most vividly. Perhaps it's predominant at the nostrils, perhaps at the chest or abdomen. Then rest your attention lightly—as lightly as a butterfly rests on a flower—on just that area.

Become aware of sensations there. If you're focusing on the breath at the nostrils, for example, you may experience tingling, vibration, pulsing. You may observe that the breath is cooler when it comes in through the nostrils and warmer

* *Visit hayhouse.co.uk/download to download this meditation (see Contents page for further instructions).*

when it goes out. If you're focusing on the breath at the abdomen, you may feel movement, pressure, stretching, release. You don't need to name these sensations—simply feel them.

Let your attention rest on the feeling of the natural breath, one breath at a time. (Notice how often the word *rest* comes up in this instruction? This is a very restful practice.) You don't need to make the breath deeper or longer or different from the way it is. Simply be aware of it, one breath at a time.

During the course of this meditation session, you may find that the rhythm of your breathing changes. Just allow it to

TRY THIS
Read First, Then Sit

Perhaps you're asking yourself, *Should I be following along, performing each action described as I read about it? What happens when I close my eyes—do I peek at the instructions?* Good questions. Four of the meditations in this book are also available on the audio download, so you can close your eyes and listen to my voice guiding you through the practice, if you wish. But I suggest that before you try each meditation exercise you read the instructions through completely a couple of times so you can absorb them and know what to expect.

And if you get lost at any point while you're doing one of the meditations, remember these simple, basic guidelines: Breathe naturally and focus on the sensations of each breath. If you have a thought or a feeling, notice it and then gently return to following your breath.

be however it is. Sometimes people get a little self-conscious, almost panicky, about watching themselves breathe—they start hyperventilating a little, or holding their breath without fully realizing what they're doing. If that happens, just breathe more gently. To help support your awareness of the breath, you might want to experiment with silently saying to yourself *in* with each inhalation and *out* with each exhalation, or perhaps *rising . . . falling.* But make this mental note very quietly within, so that you don't disrupt your concentration on the sensations of the breath.

Many distractions will arise—thoughts, images, emotions, aches, pains, plans. Just be with your breath and let them go. You don't need to chase after them, you don't need to hang on to them, you don't need to analyze them. You're just breathing. Connecting to your breath when thoughts or images arise is like spotting a friend in a crowd: You don't have to shove everyone else aside or order them to go away; you just direct your attention, your enthusiasm, your interest toward your friend. *Oh,* you think, *there's my friend in that crowd. Oh, there's my breath, among those thoughts and feelings and sensations.*

If distractions arise that *are* strong enough to take your attention away from the feeling of the breath—physical sensations, emotions, memories, plans, an incredible fantasy, a pressing list of chores, whatever it might be—or if you find that you've dozed off, don't be concerned. See if you can let go of any distractions and return your attention to the feeling of the breath.

Once you've noticed whatever has captured your attention, you don't have to do anything about it. Just be aware of it without adding anything to it—without tacking on judgment *(I fell asleep! What an idiot!)*, without interpretation *(I'm terrible at meditation)*, without comparisons *(Probably everyone trying this exercise can stay with the breath longer than I can!* Or *I should be thinking better thoughts!)*, and without projections into the future *(What if this thought irritates me so much I can't get back to concentrating on my breath? I'm going to be annoyed for the rest of my life! I'm never going to learn how to meditate!)*.

You don't have to get mad at yourself for having a thought; you don't have to evaluate its content: just acknowledge it. You're not elaborating on the thought or feeling; you're not judging it. You're neither struggling against it nor falling into its embrace and getting swept away by it. When you notice that your mind is not on your breath, notice what *is* on your mind. And then, no matter what it is, let go of it. Come back to focusing on your nostrils or your abdomen or wherever you feel your breath.

The moment you realize you've been distracted is the magic moment. It's a chance to be really different, to try a new response—rather than tell yourself you're weak or undisciplined, or give up in frustration, simply let go and begin again. In fact, instead of chastising yourself, you might thank yourself for recognizing that you've been distracted, and for returning to your breath. This act of beginning again is the essential art of the meditation practice.

Every time you find yourself speculating about the future, replaying the past, or getting wrapped up in self-criticism, shepherd your attention back to the actual sensations of the breath. (If it will help you restore concentration, mentally say

TRY THIS

Cradling the Breath

Sometimes in my own practice I use the image of holding
something very fragile, very precious, as if I had something
made of glass in my hand. If I were to grab it too tightly, it would
shatter and break, but if I were to get lazy or negligent, my hand
would open and the fragile object would fall and break. So I
just cradle it, I'm in touch with it, I cherish it. That's the way we
can be with each breath. We don't want to grab it too tightly
or be too loose; too energized or too relaxed. We meet and
cherish this moment, this breath, one breath at a time.

in . . . out with each breath, as I suggested above.) Our practice is to let go gently and return to focusing on the breath.
Note the word *gently*. We gently acknowledge and release distractions, and gently forgive ourselves for having wandered.
With great kindness to ourselves, we once more return our
attention to the breath.

If you have to let go of distractions and begin again thousands of times, fine. That's not a roadblock to the practice—that
is the practice. That's life: starting over, one breath at a time.

If you feel sleepy, sit up straighter, open your eyes if
they're closed, take a few deep breaths, and then return to
breathing naturally. You don't need to control the breath or
make it different from the way it is. Simply be with it. Feel the
beginning of the in-breath and the end of it; the beginning

of the out-breath and the end of it. Feel the little pause at the beginning and end of each breath.

Continue following your breath—and starting over when you're distracted—until you've come to the end of the time period you've set aside for meditation. When you're ready, open your eyes or lift your gaze.

Try to bring some of the qualities of concentration you just experienced—presence, calm observation, willingness to start over, and gentleness—to the next activity that you perform at home, at work, among friends, or among strangers.

HEARING MEDITATION

Sit comfortably or lie down, with your eyes closed or open; if they're open, find a spot in front of you on which to rest your gaze. Center your attention on the feeling of your breathing, wherever it's predominant, wherever it's easiest for you—just normal, natural breath. Follow your breath for a few minutes. Then turn your attention from focusing on the breath to focusing on hearing the sounds around you.

Some sounds are near and some far; some welcome (wind chimes, say, or snatches of music) some not so welcome (a car alarm, a power drill, an argument on the street). In either case, they're simply sounds arising and passing away. Whether they're soothing or jangly, you note the sounds and let them go.

There's nothing you have to do about these sounds; you can hear them without any sort of effort at all. You don't

CLOSING YOUR PRACTICE, OPENING YOUR HEART

Here's an optional way to end any meditation in this book:

As you come to the close of your practice session, feel the pleasure that comes from caring for yourself, paying attention, taking risks, and being willing to begin again. To do so isn't conceited or vain; you're experiencing the joy of making healthy choices.

And because the inner work we do is never for ourselves alone, make a point of offering the positive energy you generate in your practice to those who have helped you. Maybe it is someone who took care of things at home so you'd have more free time or someone who has been encouraging you in your practice. You can offer the energy, the positive force, the sense of possibility you've been generating to this person, so that the work you do within is for them as well. *May my practice be dedicated to your well-being.*

Maybe someone you know is hurting. The greater awareness, sensitivity, love, and kindness you're developing can be dedicated to their happiness as well. Or think of your family and the greater community. Every step we take toward peace and understanding affects everyone around us.

At the end of your meditation, say to yourself, *May the actions that I take toward the good, toward understanding myself, toward being more peaceful be of benefit to all beings everywhere.*

And when you feel ready, you can open your eyes.

need to respond to them (unless, of course, it's the sound of a smoke alarm, or your child crying); you don't need to judge them, manipulate them, or stop them. You don't even have to understand them or be able to name them. See if you can just hear a sound without naming or interpreting it. Notice changes in intensity or volume as the sound washes through you, without interference, without judgment—just arising and subsiding, arising and subsiding.

If you find yourself shrinking from a sound or wishing it were over, note that and see if you can be with it in an open, patient way. Keep your body relaxed. If the sound is upsetting, return to following your breath for a few minutes. Don't strain to hear, just stay open for the next sound.

If you find yourself craving more of a sound, take a deep breath and relax. Simply notice that a sound has arisen, that you have a certain response to it, and that there's a little space between those two events. Stay open for the next sound, recognizing that sound is continually coming and going outside of our control. If you find yourself getting tense in response to a sound, take a deep breath and relax, using whatever technique works for you; maybe it's directing breath into a tight area of the body. Or you can, at any point, return to following your breath as an anchor, as a reminder of easy, spacious relaxation. If thoughts come up, notice them and let them go. You don't have to elaborate: *Oh, that's a bus. I wonder what number? I wish they'd change the route so it's more convenient. I wish I didn't have to ride a bus at all. I'm so annoyed that my car's in the shop . . .* All you have to do is hear. All you have to do is be present.

And when you feel ready, you can open your eyes.

As you return to your daily activities, consider the way this meditation reminds us that we can meet experiences with more presence and centeredness.

LETTING GO OF THOUGHTS MEDITATION*

Michelangelo was once asked how he would carve an elephant. He replied, "I would take a large piece of stone and take away everything that was not the elephant." Practicing concentration during a meditation session is something like learning to recognize what is "not the elephant": It's a continual letting go of that which is nonessential or distracting. When we're practicing concentration and a thought arises in the mind—a memory, a plan, a comparison, an inviting fantasy—we let go of it. If anger arises, or self-judgment, or eager anticipation of a party we're going to that night, we simply let it go, calmly returning to the object of concentration. We release a thought or a feeling not because we are afraid of it or because we can't bear to acknowledge it as a part of our experience, but because in this context, it is unnecessary. Right now we are practicing concentration, sustaining our attention on the breath.

In this meditation you can sit comfortably or lie down. Close your eyes, or if you're keeping them open, find a spot in front of you to rest your gaze. Center your attention on

*Visit hayhouse.co.uk/download to download this meditation (see Contents page for further instructions).

the feeling of the in-and-out breath, at the nostrils, chest, or abdomen—just the normal, natural breath. As you feel the sensations of the breath, make a very quiet mental notation of *breath, breath* with both the in-breath and the out-breath. When a thought arises that's strong enough to take your attention away from the breath, simply note it as *not breath*. Whether it's the most beautiful thought in the world or the most terrible, one you'd never disclose to another soul, in this meditation, it's simply *not breath*.

You don't have to judge yourself; you don't have to get lost in making up a story about what triggered the thought or its possible consequences. All you have to do is recognize that it's not the breath. Some of your thoughts may be tender and caring, some may be cruel and hurtful, some may be boring and banal; all that matters is that they're not the breath. See them, recognize them, very gently let them go, and bring your attention back to the feeling of the breath.

Our habitual tendency is either to grab on to a thought and perhaps build a complicated scenario around it, or to push it away and struggle against it. In this meditation, we encounter thoughts and stay detached, centered, and calm. We simply recognize *It's not the breath* and very gently let the thought go, returning our attention to what *is* the breath.

And when you feel ready, you can open your eyes and relax.

MINI-MEDITATIONS
THROUGHOUT THE DAY

Ordinary life activities offer a chance for small bursts of meditation, times when you can shake off distraction or anxiety and restore concentration and calm.

Anywhere we happen to be breathing, we can be meditating—standing in line at the DMV, watching our kid's soccer game, before going into an important meeting. A few times a day, wherever you are, take a moment or two to tune in to the feeling of your breath at the nostrils, chest, or abdomen, whichever is most comfortable for you. You don't have to close your eyes, look odd, or feel self-conscious. You're just grabbing a quick, centering moment—as short as following three breaths—to connect with a deeper sense of yourself.

Some people set up routines or choose cues in order to build these moments of mindfulness into their day: They take three mindful breaths before they answer an e-mail; or stop and follow the breath for a few moments when the microwave dings as they're heating up their lunch; or they let the phone ring three times before they pick it up, and take a mindful, centering breath in that brief interval. I heard about one executive who has her assistant put a free minute on the calendar before every meeting for a short following-the-breath break. These moments of stealth meditation may restore the calm state we achieve in longer practice sessions, and they remind us that the breath is always there as a resource, to center us so we remember what matters.

REFLECTIONS ON WEEK ONE

The practice of feeling your breath and bringing your attention back again and again may not be glamorous or dramatic, but it makes a difference in those times when you have to say to yourself, "I need to start over. I can't just stay stuck in this place." This is a wonderful skill to bring to your life.

When I started practicing meditation, I assumed that taming the mind and developing concentration took a great deal of grim, laborious effort. At the first meditation retreat I ever attended, I became so frustrated with trying to pay attention that, in a frenzy, I declared to myself that the next time my attention wandered I would just bang my head against the wall.

Fortunately the lunch bell rang just then. Standing in the meal line, I overheard a conversation between two students I didn't know. One was asking the other how his morning had gone. The tall, thin man replied with great buoyancy of spirit, "I couldn't really concentrate very well, but this afternoon may be better."

That startled me, and I turned around to get a better look at this guy. *Why isn't he as upset as I am?* I thought. *Doesn't he take this stuff seriously at all?* This was my first meeting with Joseph Goldstein.

Five years later Joseph and I, along with Jack Kornfield and other committed friends, founded the Insight Meditation Society. By that time, I'd come to understand what lay behind Joseph's lighthearted statement. I'd learned, as my practice evolved, that the conditions required for concentration to develop were far from the sort of tormented battle I'd engaged in. Straining to attain calm makes no sense, yet that's often what we do. I realized that struggling to keep the mind on an object such as the breath doesn't create the conditions in which concentration most readily arises. When the mind is at ease, however, when our hearts are calm and open and confident, we can more comfortably, naturally concentrate. But how do we arrive at this state of ease?

It helps to have the perspective Joseph had in that lunch line so many years ago. He accepted that there are always ups and downs in meditative practice, as there are in life. Sometimes meditation is easy, fun, even ecstatic. Sometimes it's annoying, difficult, painful. Whatever it is, we stick with it: Effort needn't be struggling or straining—it can be relaxed perseverance.

Those inevitable up-and-down cycles don't need to define our sense of progress in meditation. You can't bully yourself into awareness; kindness and acceptance work much better. When thoughts and feelings distract us during our meditation session, we acknowledge them without judging

TRY THIS

Mix It Up

Experiment with the variations on the Core Meditation. On some of your practice days, use them in place of the Core Meditation. Or incorporate into your daily practice just those components you find helpful. You might, for example, choose to switch from following the breath to hearing sounds whenever you feel tense or anxious during your practice. Or you might decide to employ the mental note *not breath* when you feel especially distracted. Use whatever works for you.

them, and we let them go. This view doesn't make us undiscriminating or complacent. Rather, we capture the energy previously used to blame ourselves and direct it toward making informed choices about how we want to relate to what has come up in our minds.

Instead of being discouraged if you feel sleepy, anxious, or distracted when you wanted to feel peaceful and focused, remember that success in meditation is measured not in terms of what is happening to us but by how we relate to what is happening. Do you calmly observe your sleepiness, anxiety, or distraction? Success. Do you try to stop punishing yourself for feeling these things? Success.

The theologian and civil rights leader Howard Thurman recommended that we "look at the world with quiet eyes." It's an intriguing phrase. Too often, we're more like those cartoon creatures whose eyes are popping out on springs: "I see something I want! Give it to me!" *Boing!* "Wait—I see something better; I want that instead!" *Boing!* We grab the object, the person, the rush, and clamp on to keep it from changing or leaving. And then—*boing*—we yearn for something else, because we aren't even really paying attention to what we're grasping so tightly.

Not paying attention keeps us in an endless cycle of wanting. We move on to the next thing because we aren't really taking in what we already have; inattention creates an escalating need for stimulation. When we're keenly aware of what's happening, we don't need to grasp for the next great moment of sensation or taste or sound (all the while missing what's actually here, right in front of us). Nor do we need to postpone our feeling of happiness until a more exciting or more pleasing object comes along, thinking, *This is OK, but it would be better if . . .* Only when we are attentive in each moment do we find satisfaction in our lives. The point of our practice is to point us to our direct experience.

When we live without awareness, numb to small delights, we may more easily fall into addictive behavior, as we need increasing levels of stimulating sensations, either pleasant or painful, in order to feel alive. In the poem "Escapist—Never," Robert Frost writes,

> His life is a pursuit of a pursuit forever.
> It is the future that creates his present.
> All is an interminable chain of longing.

When our lives feel like an interminable chain of longing—when nothing satisfies us the way we thought it might—often the first link in the chain is not being fully present. Here's how it works: Imagine eating an apple. If you do so paying very little attention to the sight of it, the feel, the smell and the taste, then eating the apple isn't likely to be a fulfilling experience. Becoming aware of a mild discontent, you're likely to blame the apple for being boring and commonplace. It's easy to miss the fact that the quality of your attention played a major role in your dissatisfaction.

You may begin to think, *If only I could have a banana, then I'd be happy!* You find a banana, but you eat it in the same distracted or inattentive way, so again you end up feeling unsatisfied. But instead of realizing that you weren't paying attention to the experience of eating the banana, you start to think, *My life is just too prosaic; how could anybody be happy with apples and bananas? What I need is something exotic. I need a mango. Then I'll be happy.*

With some effort, you find your mango. The first few bites are wonderful; this is a fresh sensation. You proclaim it delicious, just what you were looking for. Soon, however, you're finishing off the exotic mango in just the same distracted, preoccupied way you ate the prosaic apple and the banana, and once again you're left with a feeling of dissatisfaction, of yearning. It's not the fault of the apple, the banana, or the mango. It's the quality of your attention that's driving

TRY THIS
Keep a Sitting Journal

Each time you meditate, record in a small notebook how long you practiced and the predominant aspect of your meditation—a few quick notes, such as "sleepy," or "couldn't stop planning for tomorrow," or "clear and energized," or "wished I were skiing." Then at night add a word or two describing your general emotional state that day—"impatient," say, or "resolved," "openhearted," "calm and confident," "anxious." At the end of every week, review your journal and see if you notice a relationship between your sitting and the rest of your day.

your quest for something more. That's how an "interminable chain of longing" gets forged. Concentration is what breaks the chain.

Learning to deepen our concentration allows us to look at the world with quiet eyes. We don't need to reach out and grab ever more exotic or forbidden fruit. We develop calm and tranquility—and the calmer we get, the more at home we feel with our body and mind, with life as it is.

FAQs

Q. **I find it very hard to concentrate on my breath. Am I doing something wrong?**

A. Being with the breath isn't easy to do. To explain the proper technique for focusing attention on the breath, I often use the image of trying to pick up a piece of broccoli with a fork. Your goal is connecting the fork with the broccoli just deeply enough so that you can lift it to your mouth. To accomplish this, you need two things. The first is aim: If you wave the fork around in the air without homing in on a target, you won't get a lot to eat. The second is a careful modulation of energy. If you're too listless, the fork will hang in your hand; if you're too forceful and bash at the broccoli, food and plate will go flying. Either way, you won't get any nourishment. So we aim our attention toward just this one breath and simply connect.

TRY THIS

Counting the Breath

A practical tactic: If mentally saying *in . . . out*, or *rising . . . falling* as you inhale and exhale doesn't help you aim your attention, try counting the breath. As you breathe in, make a silent mental note of "in." And as you breathe out, note, "one." So, with the breath, it's "in," "one." "In," "two." "In," three," and so on. The numbering should be very quiet, with your attention really on the feeling of the breath. When you get up to ten, you can begin again with one. If you're human, you're likely to get lost in fantasy or entangled in a train of thought before you hit two or three. As soon as you realize your mind has wandered, just go back to one and start again with the next breath. Starting over doesn't imply failure. It's just a method of support for deepening concentration.

One of my teachers had a trick question he asked students during meditation retreats: "How many breaths can you be with before your mind starts to wander?" People want to be able to say, "I can be with the breath for forty-five minutes or an hour before I get lost in thought." But really, we can be with two, three, maybe four breaths before our attention starts to wander to the past, to the future, to judgment, to analysis, to fantasy. The question is: What happens in the moment when you recognize that your mind has wandered? Can you gently let go and return your attention to the present moment, to feeling your breath? The real key to being with your breath is being able to begin again.

Q When I try to meditate, I become so conscious of the breath that I almost hyperventilate. How do I just breathe normally?

A When I was a beginner, I found that every time I began one breath, I would already be anticipating the next. Leaning forward was the habit of my mind; I was very wary and concerned about what would happen next in life, and I brought that hypervigilance into meditation practice. I had so much performance anxiety that I couldn't concentrate on my breath. What I needed was to settle back in my mind and let the breath come.

But sometimes we settle back too far, get too relaxed, and that's when we get sleepy or bored or distracted. We almost lose interest in the breath. When that happens, we need to rev up our energy—take more of an interest in the process of breathing, refocus, reconnect. One way to do that might be to give yourself a little challenge: See if you can feel the end of one breath and the beginning of the next.

Losing and restoring balance is part of the practice. The trick always is to begin again—to realize that nothing is ruined when we lose track of our breath.

Q I really can't stop thinking when I meditate. Isn't meditation supposed to get rid of thoughts?

A The point of meditation is not to annihilate thoughts; obviously there are plenty of times in life when thinking is called for—vital, in fact, to our survival. What we hope to learn is the difference between thinking and being lost in thought. We don't want to stop our thoughts but to change our relationship with them—to be more present and aware when we're thinking. If we're aware of what we're thinking, if we see clearly what's going on in our minds, then we can choose whether and how to act on our thoughts.

Furthermore, you could have the most vile, terrible thoughts and you'd still have a good meditation session, depending on how spacious you are with those thoughts— that is, how much room you give them just to be, how closely you observe them, how forgiving of yourself you are. As several teachers of mindfulness have said, "Thoughts aren't facts." And thoughts aren't acts. They're just thoughts, part of the passing mental landscape. Thoughts moving through your mind are like clouds moving across the sky. They are not the sky, and the sky remains unchanged by them. The way to be with them is just to watch them go by. That's not generally how we experience our thoughts, but that's what you're working toward. I also like the image of the mind Dan Siegel, M.D., co-director of UCLA's Mindful Awareness Research Center, uses in his book *Mindsight:* "The mind is like the ocean . . . no matter what the surface conditions are like, whether it's smooth or choppy . . . deep in the ocean it's tranquil and serene. From the depth of the ocean, you can look toward the surface and simply notice the activities there, just as from the depth of the mind you can look upward toward . . . all that activity of mind—the thoughts, feelings, sensations, and memories."

Both vivid images point to the same fact: Thoughts and feelings move through our minds and constantly change; they're not who we are. They're just what we're thinking and feeling in the moment.

Q **What happens when I want to empty my mind but no matter what I do, I keep obsessing about a particular person?**

A First, it's important not to blame yourself for having these thoughts. I learned a valuable lesson from one of my earliest teachers in India. I went to him in great distress because I'd had jealous thoughts during meditation. "Why are you so upset about the thought that came up in your mind?" he said. "Did you invite it?" That was eye-opening. Do we say to ourselves, *At five o'clock I'd like to be filled with self-hatred and regret?* Of course not. Just notice the thoughts and sensations very briefly, and move on, returning to the breath. The point isn't to condemn yourself for the content of your thought; it's to recognize the thought, observe it, let it go, and return to following your breath.

Q **I start out okay, I really get rolling—then it seems I'm back to square one, and I can't concentrate at all. Will I ever make progress?**

A My early meditation practice was extremely painful, physically and emotionally. But then I went through a phase of experiencing real delight. I would sit, follow my

THE CHATTERING MIND

In our everyday lives, when we aren't attentive and mindful, we very often get swept up in a chain of associations and lose touch with what's happening in the here and now. The same thing can happen during meditation, and it's useful to observe that process in microcosm. Here's a snapshot of ten minutes in the life of a typical meditator:

You're sitting and feeling your breath, and you think, *I wonder what's for lunch?* And that leads to another thought: *Maybe I should become a vegetarian, because it would be better for my health and more in tune with my values.* And then you're off and running: *Okay, I'll be a vegetarian. But it's hard to be a vegetarian, unless you're a really good cook. I'll go to a bookstore the instant this sitting is over and buy a bunch of vegetarian cookbooks. And while I'm there, I think I'll get a book on Mexico, because I really want to go to Mexico on my next vacation. No, wait—now that I meditate and I'm a vegetarian, I'll go to India! What should be my first stop?* You wake up in Delhi—and the last thing you remember thinking was, *What's for lunch?*

Our objective when we meditate is to know what we're thinking as we're thinking it, and to know what we're feeling as we're feeling it instead of mentally ending up on another continent, wondering how we got there. When waves of memories, plans, and random thinking seem overwhelming, focus on breathing softly without forcing the breath. This will begin to settle your mind.

breath, and feel as if I were floating in the air, my mind serene. *Oh,* I would think, *isn't it going to be wonderful living the entire rest of my life in this lovely state?*

But then my knee would start hurting, or my back would ache, or I'd feel restless or sleepy, and I'd chastise myself: *What did you do wrong to make that beautiful, extraordinary state go away?*

In fact, it didn't go away because I did anything wrong: It went away because everything goes away. Every sensation, every emotion, is changing all of the time. Each experience, however intense, is ephemeral. All of life is transitory. Observing the ebb and flow of thoughts and feelings teaches us to embrace this truth.

Square one isn't such a bad place to be. Any meditation, even one in which you catch yourself getting distracted, or feeling bad, is a useful one.

Q How do I keep from nodding off in meditation?

A Don't worry about dozing; it's going to happen. Part of meditation is the burgeoning of calm and tranquility, part of it is an increase of energy, and the two aren't always in synch. Inevitably there'll be times when the calm side is deepening but you're not generating enough energy to match it. That's not a bad state, just an imbalanced one—and it will make you drowsy.

You can deal with sleepiness in a variety of skillful ways. One is accepting that it's an impermanent state. It comes and goes; you'll get past it. Another is approaching the sleepiness with openhearted acceptance and observing it closely. Thinking of it as an enemy only makes you feel worse; you are piling tension and animosity on top of fatigue. Try being with the drowsiness and observing its different components. Where do you feel the fatigue? Are your eyes drooping, your limbs heavy? Is your head falling forward? How many signs of drowsiness can you spot? Has your breath changed? Your posture? Taking an interest in your drowsiness and investigating it is likely to wake you up.

You can also take some practical steps to pick up your energy. One of my Indian teachers would frequently ask students how our practice was going. At that point I was falling

TRY THIS
Touch Points

Here's an anchoring exercise you can use if your mind is wandering and following your breath isn't helping: Become aware of your body's touch points—the small areas, about the size of a quarter, where your back, thighs, knees, or buttocks are in contact with the chair or cushion, your hand is in contact with your knee, your lips are touching, your ankles are crossed. In the small gap between your in-breath and out-breath, focus on these points of contact; picture them, feel them. Doing so may pull you away from your spiraling thoughts and bring you back to this moment, this breath.

asleep frequently in meditation, and I was very anxious about anyone finding out. But when the teacher asked the woman next to me how she was doing, she told him unself-consciously, "Oh, I fall asleep all the time." I was so relieved! And then instead of an esoteric response, the teacher simply said: "Try standing up, or throwing some cold water on your face"—very practical suggestions to change the energy balance. You can also try sitting with your eyes open, or stepping outside for a moment when you start to nod off. Over time, your practice will deepen; you'll find balance, and you won't be so sleepy.

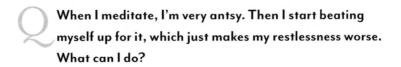

When I meditate, I'm very antsy. Then I start beating myself up for it, which just makes my restlessness worse. What can I do?

Restlessness is the flip side of drowsiness, a signal that our system is out of balance because of a tranquility deficit. A student once asked me, "Has anyone ever died of restlessness?" I told her, "Not from just one moment at a time of it." And luckily, that's how *everything* happens—one moment at a time.

If your restlessness is taking you away from following your breath, make the restlessness the temporary object of your meditation. The first thing to do is look for what you're adding on to the restless feeling—those secondary thoughts like, *I shouldn't be feeling this. This is no good. I'm so out of control. Everyone else is in control. I'm the only one who isn't. If only I were stronger (more patient, smarter, kinder), I wouldn't feel this way*. When you're in high-energy mode, it's easy to go off on a judgment jag. Instead of chastising yourself, try observing the physical sensations that accompany these thoughts and the emotions that arise; notice them and name them. Perhaps restlessness is composed of frustration, boredom, fear, annoyance.

Another very different approach to restlessness is balancing the energy by giving it room to move. That might mean sitting with your eyes open instead of closed, or listening to sounds come and go, or finding ways to make your mind feel more expansive, such as looking at the space in the room instead of the objects, or feeling your whole body sitting in space. It might mean switching to a walking meditation (see Week Two, page 81). It might mean going outside and looking at the sky.

One of the things I realized in my practice was that my restlessness often took the form of incessant planning. I'd watch these thoughts carefully, trying not to judge them, and after the meditation session, I would reflect more fully on what had come up. I came to see that I was operating on the belief that if I could just plan things thoroughly enough, I could control them and make them happen. Planning made me feel secure. The insight I gained from closely observing my restlessness during meditation led me later to examine the anxiety behind my overplanning.

As I related to these emotions with compassion, I began to release the worry and restlessness that were taking me away from the present moment, both in meditation and in my daily life. Perhaps you'll find such useful information when you explore your restlessness and observe the emotions that come up during your sessions. But save the analysis and probing for after meditation.

These two opposites—sleepiness and restlessness—are normal experiences. Especially at the beginning of a meditation period, as you enter into stillness, you may feel as if you have two voices in your head. One says, *Nothing's happening here, might as well sleep* and the other says *Nothing's happening here, let's make something happen.* Either you can't keep your eyes open, or you're wired, your mind flooded with ideas and plans. Both conditions can be quite instructive, and are temporary.

Q **When I'm sitting and feel stiffness in my knees, should I adjust my posture, or just keep focusing on my breathing?**

A First make sure you're not sitting in a position that strains your body. If the discomfort gets too intrusive, you should change position, maybe sit differently. You could be uncomfortable in the new, unfamiliar position you're assuming. What sometimes happens to people new to meditation is that in the silence and stillness of sitting, you suddenly become aware of aches and twinges that you always have but don't notice during your busy, active day. Also, deeply held tension can surface when you start clearing your mind and focusing on body sensations. If you find that you're fighting the pain, hating it, it's better to change your posture and begin again as though it's a new sitting.

OFF THE CUSHION: EXERCISES FOR PRACTICING CONCENTRATION

WORKING WITH THE UNINVITED THOUGHT

When focusing our attention in meditation, we may notice that one or two distracting thoughts keep cycling back into our mind. Let's investigate one of those now. Did a specific person or scenario resurface this week? Did you habitually make a plan, relive a conversation, or anticipate a future event? Envision that situation. Can you find an emotion that is driving it? Perhaps anxiety, or anticipation, or a concern your needs won't be met. Rather than circle around the thoughts, we can go deeper to see what's behind them.

LOOK AT YOURSELF WITH QUIET EYES

Non-judgment can be a valuable teaching tool when incorporated into our favorite activities. Set aside time to garden, bike, hike, read, cook, craft, or do any hobby you genuinely enjoy. Pick a minimum amount of time you'll do this without multitasking, and set a timer to hold yourself to it. Put down your phone, turn off the TV, and be completely present. Notice the sounds, sights, and tactile sensations the activity brings. Do not judge your process or the outcome. If you find your mind wandering, return to the present task. When the timer rings, ponder what felt different when you applied mindfulness to the task.

JOURNAL PROMPT FOR REFLECTION

EMBRACING THE DISTRACTIONS

We're learning that distractions can come from internal thoughts or external surroundings. List distractions you've noticed in meditation this week. Now, list anything you identify that habitually pulls focus throughout your day. What was the moment like that you let go of those distractions? Could you do that gently, or did you find yourself being critical or judgmental? Putting your experience on paper might help you remember to be kind to yourself when faced with these distractions in the future.

THE TAKEAWAY

Meditation is a microcosm, a model, and a mirror. The skills we practice when we sit are transferable to the rest of our lives. In Week One we used the tool of concentration to steady and focus the mind. Following the breath, we became aware of thoughts, feelings, and sensations. We noted them and let them go without getting swept away by them, without dodging them or ignoring them (as we might normally have done in our busy daily lives), and without berating ourselves for having them. Such a small act can have big reverberations.

Conventional ideas about meditation say we're succeeding when we can go from following one breath to following fifty before our attention wanders. But this is what success actually looks and feels like in this process:

We learn how to stay in the moment. As we follow the breath, our attention wanders; we catch ourselves and come back to the current breath—not the one that just left our body, or the one to come. For a few seconds, perhaps, we're nowhere else but with that breath. Now we have a template for the feeling of complete attention in the present moment. A student once told me, "I was on vacation, hiking in Bryce Canyon, and on the very first day I started thinking about how much I was going to hate leaving and going back to work. I got so caught up in mourning the end of the trip that I wasn't even paying attention to this place I love so much—I might as well have been back in the office. Then I sort of saw myself being spun away by my thoughts—I even said *thinking, thinking* to myself—and I let them go. I told myself to start over, and be where I was—a much better place than the future. Before I started meditating, I would have just gone on down the rapids and over the falls with my thinking, and missed the vacation I was having because I was already brooding over going back home."

We practice letting go of judgments. As a beginning meditator, I certainly had a tendency to judge the way I was performing this new task: *My breath isn't good enough, deep enough, broad enough, subtle enough, clear enough.* I found that I loaded on to the simple act of breathing all sorts of pronouncements and projections about what kind of person I was. Returning to the breath, continually letting go of these judgments, gave birth to compassion for myself.

We become aware of a calm, stable center that can steady us even when our lives are in upheaval. The better you get at concentrating your attention on the chosen object, the breath, the deeper the stillness and calm you feel. As your mind withdraws from obsessive thinking, fruitless worry, and self-recrimination, you feel a sense of refuge. You have a safe place to go, and it's within.

One meditation student described accessing that center when she stopped working full-time to stay home and care for her aged mother, who suffered from dementia. Even with the help of her husband and children, she said, the task was overwhelming, and overwhelmingly sad. After several months, she felt hopeless and exhausted. "We couldn't afford to put my mom in a good-quality nursing home, and because her physical health was okay, I pictured this state of affairs going on for a long time. I couldn't imagine how I would manage years in this draining, demanding situation. I felt paralyzed and sort of hysterical. But I stopped and followed my breath, the way I'd learned, and then I just did what I had to do next. I didn't think about the rest of my mom's life, just the next task, the next moment. One moment at a time was doable. And I was able to remind myself that if I have resentful feelings or frustrated ones, it doesn't mean I'm a bad person. I felt much better knowing that I could always stop and find some calmness and strength in my breath. I knew I wanted to do this for my mother, and I knew I could."

We become kinder to ourselves. Every time we get distracted and then start over without chiding ourselves, we're practicing compassion. Meditation teaches us gentleness with ourselves and the ability to forgive our mistakes and move on.

With true calm comes new energy. The inner quiet engendered by concentration isn't passive or sluggish; nor is it coldly distant from your experience—it is vital and alive. It creates a calm infused with energy, alertness, and interest. You can fully connect to what's happening in your life, have a bright and clear awareness of it, yet be relaxed. People tell me they're surprised that just twenty minutes of practice a day can begin to create this change. One new meditator, a grocery store produce manager, told me, "After a month of meditating, I just felt peppier—even though I could hardly stay awake for it at first. I think it was because I was always running in a million different directions at once, starting a bunch of projects and never feeling as if I gave any of them my full attention, and I didn't realize how tiring that was. Also, keeping my feelings at a distance—trying to bury anger and frustration, instead of feeling them—must have been really hard work. I stopped doing that little by little, because the instruction in meditation was not to judge myself. Maybe that's part of why I don't feel so tired."

We become more self-reliant. Because the development of this inner calm and energy happens completely within and isn't dependent on another person or a particular situation, we begin to feel a resourcefulness and independence that is quite beautiful—and a huge relief. We see that we don't have to look outside of ourselves for a sense of fulfillment. Such calm, composed strength is its own special type of happiness.

Mindfulness and the Body

LETTING GO OF BURDENS

D EVELOPING OUR CONCENTRATION helps us steady our attention. The next skill we'll develop, mindfulness, helps us to free our attention from burdens we may not even know we're hauling around.

The first time a meditation teacher encouraged me to practice mindfulness—which entails giving purposeful, nonjudgmental attention to whatever arises in the present moment—I made a discovery. As I focused my attention not only on each breath but also on any thought, emotion, or physical sensation that came up while I was sitting, I began to notice that with each experience, two things were happening. There was the actual experience and then there was what I was adding on to it because of habitual responses that I'd developed over a lifetime.

One of the first places I saw this happening was in my knees. My teacher encouraged his students not to move during our sittings. I, however, always moved; my knees hurt; so did my back. The more I tried to be still, the more I shifted and readjusted. Eventually I realized that I moved not because the pain in my knees or back was really so severe, but because as soon as I felt one little moment of discomfort, I'd start thinking, *What's it going to feel like in ten minutes? In twenty minutes? It's going to be unbearable.* So I'd change positions, motivated not by present discomfort, but by anticipated pain. I was imagining aches multiplied by minutes, hours, years, until I felt them as a burden too impossibly big for anyone to bear. And then I'd spiral into self-judgment: *Why did you move? You didn't have to move. You're always the first to move.*

The disruption to my concentration from moving lasted only thirty seconds, but the disruption from anxiously imagining the future and then unleashing all those rebukes added another ten minutes of mental distress. Until I learned to spot those add-ons—a tendency to judge myself harshly and to spin a permanently miserable future from a temporary sensation—they came between me and my direct experience: *This is what knee pain feels like right now, not an hour from now. It's throbbing, needle-like. Now it's little spasms, with a still space between them. . . . Can I handle it for right now? Yes, I can.* Only direct experience gives us the crucial information we need to know what is actually happening.

Mindfulness, also called wise attention, helps us see what we're adding to our experiences, not only during meditation sessions but also elsewhere. These add-ons might take the form of projecting into the future *(my neck hurts, so I'll be miserable forever)*, foregone conclusions *(there's no point in asking for a raise)*, rigid concepts *(you're either for me or against me)*, unexamined habits (you feel tense and reach for a cookie) or associative thinking (you snap at your daughter and then leap to your own childhood problems and then on to deciding you're just like your mom). I'm not saying we should abolish concepts or associations; that's not possible, nor is it desirable. There are times when associative thinking leads to creative problem-solving, or works of art. But we want to see clearly what we're doing as we're doing it, to be able to distinguish our direct experience from the add-ons, and to know that we can choose whether to heed them or not. Maybe there *is* no point in asking for a raise, maybe there is. You can't know until you separate your conditioned assumption—*I never get what I ask for*—from the unadorned facts of your work situation

A very good place to become familiar with the way mindfulness works is always close by—our own bodies. Investigating physical sensations is one of the best ways for us to learn to be present with whatever is happening in the moment, and to recognize the difference between direct experience and the add-ons we bring to it. Next week we'll apply the tool of mindfulness to emotions and thoughts.

I once witnessed a particularly good example of add-ons in action when I was teaching a retreat with my colleague Joseph Goldstein. We were sitting drinking tea when a student in some distress came in and said, "I just had this terrible experience." Joseph asked "What happened?" And the man said, "I was meditating and I felt all this tension in my jaw and I realized what an incredibly uptight person I am, and always have been and I always will be."

"You mean you felt some tension in your jaw," Joseph said. And the man said, "Yes. And I've never been able to get close to anyone, and I'm going to be alone for the rest of my life."

"You mean you felt tension in your jaw," said Joseph. I watched the man continue barreling down this path for some time, all because of a sore jaw, until finally Joseph said to him, "You're having a painful experience. Why are you adding a horrible self-image to it?"

I'm sure you know how the man with the sore jaw felt. We've all had times when we've declared ourselves total losers or envisioned a bad end based on a fleeting sensation or thought. A typical trip down that path goes like this: I bend down to tie my shoe, and somehow I pull a muscle in my back. *This is the beginning of the end,* I think. *Now everything will start to go.* (Joseph would say, "You mean you hurt your back.")

PRACTICE PREVIEW

〜〜〜

This week's mindfulness exercises—a Body Scan, a Walking Meditation, a Body Sensation Meditation, and three shorter meditations rooted in everyday experiences— will help us feel more comfortable and in tune with our bodies.

NUTS AND BOLTS

In Week Two, add a fourth day of practice, with a session of at least twenty minutes. Try to integrate both walking and sitting meditations. If you meditate in the evening and you're feeling either extra restless or drowsy, you may want to do a walking meditation as a way of rebalancing your energy. Or you may simply enjoy getting back into your body if you've been sitting at a desk and living in your head all day.

Though some of this week's meditations begin with our concentrating on the breath, as in Week One, or using the breath as an anchor to which we can return, breathing isn't always the main focus. Some don't involve awareness of the breath at all. The breath is one of the many tools for training attention; in this 28-day introductory program, my goal is to give you an overview of many different methods and techniques available to you.

They'll deepen our understanding of the way our experiences are constantly changing, and they'll help us spot our add-ons.

In the Body Sensation Meditation, for example, we'll use mindfulness to observe the way we automatically cling to pleasant experiences and push away unpleasant ones. It's natural to perceive everything we think, feel, or take in with our five senses as being pleasant, unpleasant, or neutral. Whether we're enjoying the sun on our face, hearing an insult, listening to music, smelling our dinner cooking, or feeling a wave of anger, the experience gets sorted into one of these three slots. It's just what humans do.

When the experience is pleasant, our conditioned tendency is to hang on to it and keep it from leaving. That, however, is impossible. "Nothing endures but change," said the Greek philosopher Heraclitus. We long for permanence, but everything in the known universe—thoughts, weather, people, galaxies—is transient. That's a fact, but one we fight. Mindfulness allows us to enjoy pleasant experiences without that extra thing we do, which is to grasp at the pleasure in an attempt to keep it from changing. In fact, we're often so preoccupied with trying to make a pleasurable experience stay that we're unable to enjoy it while it lasts.

I remember losing touch with mindfulness when a friend from California who'd never been East planned an autumn visit to New England. Anticipating her arrival, I anxiously worried about whether the resplendent, colorful leaves would stay beautiful for her. *It's got to be this way when she comes,* I thought. *If the leaves fall and they're all brown and shriveled, what kind of an inaugural autumn visit will that be for her?* As it turned out, she wasn't able to come after all. When I heard that, I thought, *Well, I guess now I can just let nature take its course.* Obviously, it's ludicrous to try to keep leaves from falling from the trees. And I'd been so anxious about their departure that I missed their full glory when it was right in front of me.

On the other hand, if an experience, thought, or feeling is painful, our tendency is to run from it or push it away. For example, if we have physical pain in one part of the body, we might find the rest of our body tightening up, as though to ward off further discomfort. In that way, our aversion to pain adds tension and tightness to the original discomfort. Or maybe we globalize the pain and load it with judgment and recrimination. *(This is all my fault. It will never change.)*

Ironically we might have little direct knowledge of the pain we're reacting to because we're scrambling so fast to make it leave, often in ways that make it worse. What we have to understand is that there's a big difference between pain and suffering. We can have a painful physical experience, but we don't need to add the suffering of fear or projection into the future or other mental anguish to it. Mindfulness can play a big role in transforming our experience with pain and other difficulties; it allows us to recognize the authenticity of the distress and yet not be overwhelmed by it.

And if an experience is neutral, ordinary, we tend to disconnect from it or ignore it. We live in a fog, or in our heads, oblivious to many daily moments that might offer the possibility for richness in our lives. In an ordinary day we can be moving so fast that we lose touch with quieter moments of happiness that could nourish and sustain us. Some of us may come to believe we need a dose of drama—good or bad—or a jolt of adrenaline to wake us up and make us feel alive; we get hooked on risks and thrills.

When we can't let the moment in front of us be what it is (because we're afraid that if it's good, it will end too soon; if it's bad, it'll go on forever; and if it's neutral, it'll bore us to tears), we're out of balance. Mindfulness restores that balance;

we catch our habitual reactions of clinging, condemning, and zoning out, and let them go.

BODY SCAN MEDITATION

Lie down in a comfortable spot with your arms by your sides and your eyes closed. Breathe naturally, as in the Week One Core Meditation. You are going to do a scan of the entire body from top to bottom as a way of getting centered—a reminder that you can be at home in your body. To begin, feel the floor (or the bed, or the couch) supporting you. Relax and allow yourself to be supported. Bring your attention to your back, and when you feel a spot that's tense or resisting, take a deep breath and relax.

If during your body scan you detect a sensation that's pleasant, you may feel an urge to hang on to it. If so, relax, open up, and see if you can be with the sensation of pleasure without the clinging. If you detect a sensation that's painful, you may reflexively try to push it away; you may feel angry about it, or afraid of it. If you spot any of these reactions, see if you can release them. Come back to the direct experience of the moment—what is the actual sensation of the pain or pleasure? Feel it directly, without interpretation or judgment.

Bring your attention to the top of your head and simply feel whatever sensations are there—tingling, say, or itching, pulsing; perhaps you notice an absence of sensation.

Very slowly, let your attention move down the front of your face. Be aware of whatever you encounter—tightness, relaxation, pressure; whether pleasant, painful, or neutral—in your forehead, nose, mouth, cheeks. Is your jaw clenched or loose?

Turn your attention to your eyes, and feel the weight of your eyelids, the movement of your eyeballs in their sockets, the brush of the lashes. Feel your lips, the light pressure of skin on skin, softness, moisture, coolness. You needn't name these things, just feel them. If you can, try to step out of the world of concepts like "eyelids" or "lips" and into the world of direct sensation—intimate, immediate, alive, ever-changing.

Return your attention to the top of your head, then move down the back of the head, over the curve of your skull. Notice your neck; any knots or sore spots?

Once again return to the top of the head, and then move your attention down the sides, feeling your ears, the sides of your neck, the tops of your shoulders. You don't have to judge the sensations or trade them in for different ones; just feel them.

Slowly move your awareness down the upper arms, feeling the elbows, the forearms. Let your attention rest for a moment on your hands—the palms, the backs. See if you can feel each separate finger, each fingertip.

Bring your attention back to the neck and throat, and slowly move it down through the chest, noticing any sensations you find there. Keep moving your attention downward, to the rib cage, the abdomen. Your awareness is gentle, receptive; you're not looking for anything special but rather staying open to whatever feelings you might find. You don't have to do anything about them; you're just noticing them.

Return your attention to the neck, and now let your awareness move down the back of your body: shoulder blades, the midback, the lower back. You may feel stiffness, tension, creakiness, quivering—whatever you encounter, simply notice it.

Now bring your attention into the pelvic area and see what sensations you feel there. Slowly move your awareness down your thighs, your knees, your calves, and all the way down your legs, feeling the ankles. Settle your attention into your feet.

When you feel ready, open your eyes.

As you end the meditation, see if you can continue to feel the world of sensation and all of its changes, moment by moment, as you move into the activities of your daily life.

WALKING MEDITATION*

Walking meditation is—literally—a wonderful step-by-step way of learning to be mindful and of bringing mindfulness into everyday activity. It becomes a model, a bridge, for being mindful in all the movements we make throughout the day.

The essence of walking meditation is to bring mindfulness to an act that we normally do mechanically. So often when we're getting ourselves from place to place, we're on automatic pilot, hurrying because we're looking forward to a rendezvous or late for a meeting. Maybe we're planning our excuse, imagining what the other person will say, and what

* Visit hayhouse.co.uk/download to download this meditation (see Contents page for further instructions).

our response will be. We get so caught up in the story that we miss the journey. So in this meditation we shed the story and bring our attention to the basics—the sensations of our body moving through space.

Instead of following your breath, as in the Week One Core Meditation, you'll let your attention rest fully on the sensation of your feet and legs as you lift them, move them through space, and place them on the ground. Most of the time we have the sense that our consciousness, who we are, resides in our head, somewhere behind our eyes. But in this meditation, we're going to put our feet in charge. Try to feel your feet not as if you're looking down at them, but as if they're looking up at you—as if your consciousness is emanating from the ground up.

You may practice either inside or outside. Be sure you have enough space to walk at least twenty steps, at which point you'll turn around and retrace your path. If it's possible, you can also do your walking meditation outdoors where you won't need to turn around. While you're walking, your eyes will, of course, be open, and you'll remain fully aware of your surroundings, even though your focus will be on the movement of your body.

Start by standing comfortably with your eyes open at the beginning of the path you've chosen. Your feet are shoulder-width apart, your weight evenly distributed upon them. Hold your arms at your sides in whatever way seems comfortable and natural, or clasp your hands lightly behind your back or in front of you.

Now settle your attention into your feet. Feel the tops of your feet, the soles; see if you can feel each toe. Become aware of your foot making contact with your shoes (if you're wearing them) and then the sensations of your foot making contact with the floor or ground. Do you feel heaviness, softness, hardness? Smoothness or roughness? Do you feel lightly connected to the floor or heavily grounded? Open yourself to the sensations of contact between foot and floor or ground, whatever they might be. Let go of the concepts of foot and leg and simply feel those sensations.

Still standing comfortably, begin slowly to shift your weight onto your left foot. Notice each subtle physical alteration as you redistribute your weight—changes in balance, the way your muscles stretch, strain, and relax again, any cracking or popping in your ankle. Maybe there's a little trembling in the leg bearing the weight, maybe your leg feels supple or strong.

Very slowly and carefully, begin to move back to the center, with your weight equally distributed on both feet. Then shift your weight onto your right foot and leg. Once again notice what your body feels as you make this adjustment. Be aware of the difference between the weight-bearing leg and the left leg.

Gently come back to center and stand comfortably for a moment.

Now you'll begin walking, with the same deliberate movement, the same gentle attention that you just practiced as you shifted your weight. Remain relaxed but alert and receptive. Walking at a normal speed, focus on the movement of your legs and feet. Notice that you can focus on the feeling of your

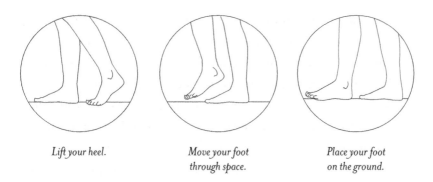

Lift your heel.   *Move your foot*   *Place your foot*
                        through space.   *on the ground.*

feet touching the ground and at the same time be aware of the sights and sounds around you without getting lost in them. It is a light attentiveness to the sensations of movement, not a tight focus. The sensations are like a touchstone for us. You can make a quiet mental note of *touch, touch.*

After a few minutes, see if you can slow down a bit and be aware of what it feels like as you lift the heel, then the whole foot; what it feels like when you move your leg through space and place your foot. Make a simple mental note each time your foot lifts and each time it touches the ground, *lift, place; lift, place* or *up, down; up, down* to anchor your attention.

If you're outside, you may find yourself distracted by people moving around you, the play of sun and shadow, the barking of a dog. That's okay; just return to focusing on your feet touching the ground. When you notice that your mind is wandering, bring your attention back to the stepping, the sensation of movement. Notice that the very moment you recognize that you've been distracted, you've already begun again to be aware.

After some minutes, slow your walking down further and divide the step into three parts: *lift, move, place* or *up, forward, down*. Finish one step completely before you lift the other foot. See if you can detect the specific sensations associated with each small part of the step: lifting the heel, lifting the whole foot, moving the leg forward, placing the foot down on the ground; the sensation of touching, of shifting your weight, of lifting the other heel, and then repeating the process. The rhythm of this slow walking is quite different from the rhythm of the way we usually move. It might take a while for you to get used to this new pace and cadence: lift, move, place, and come to rest. Only then lift the back foot.

Though your attention is on your feet and legs, you may occasionally want to check in with the rest of your body. Become aware of the sensations in your legs, hips, back—pressure, stiffness, or fluidity. No need to name them, though; just feel them. Then come back to the sensations in your feet and legs. Feel the slight bounce as your foot meets the ground and the security of the earth holding you up.

Keep the noting—*lift, move, place*—very soft and your movements graceful, as if this slow walking were a martial arts exercise, or a kind of dance step. Lift, move, place. Lift, move, place. Stay with the feeling of what you're experiencing right now, in just this moment.

Newcomers to walking meditation may feel a bit wobbly —and the more slowly you move and the more aware of your feet you become, the more unbalanced you feel. If that happens, speed up a bit. Do the same if your mind starts wandering a lot, or you're having trouble connecting with your bodily sensations. Then slow down again when your concentration is restored. Experiment with pace until you find the speed that best allows you to keep your attention on the feeling of walking —the speed that allows you to remain most mindful.

And after twenty minutes or so of walking, simply stop and stand. Notice what you feel at the point where your feet meet the floor or ground; take in what you see and hear around you. Gently end the meditation.

Remember that at any place and at any time throughout the rest of your day, you can bring mindfulness to a movement, becoming aware of how your body feels as you stand, sit, walk, climb stairs, turn, reach for the telephone, lift a fork at mealtime, or open the front door.

TRY THIS
Walking Optional

If walking is a problem for you, you can do this meditation without actually walking. Instead, sit (or lie down if you're bedridden) and focus your awareness on another part of the body—moving your hand up and down, say—or on the sensations of wheeling if you're in a wheelchair. When the instructions call for slow, deliberate, focused movements of the legs and foot, do the same with whatever part of the body you're using.

BODY SENSATIONS MEDITATION*

Sit comfortably on the floor with your legs crossed and your back straight, or lie on your back with your arms at your sides. Your eyes may be open or closed.

Begin with hearing: Be aware of any sounds that reach you. Let them come and go; you don't have to do anything about them.

Now bring the same relaxed and open awareness to your breath, at the nostrils, the chest, or the abdomen, wherever you detect it most clearly. If you wish, make a quiet mental note on each inhalation and exhalation—*in, out,* or *rising, falling.*

The breath is the primary object of awareness here until a physical sensation is strong enough to take your attention away. If that happens, rather than struggle against it, let go of the awareness of the breath, and let your attention settle fully on the bodily sensation that has distracted you. Let it become the new object of your meditation.

If it's helpful to you, make a quick, quiet mental note of whatever you're feeling, whether it's painful or pleasing: *Warmth, coolness, fluttering, itching, ease.* No need to find exactly the right words—noting just helps bring your mind into more direct contact with the actual experience. You're not trying to control what you feel in your body, nor are you trying to change it. You're simply allowing sensations to come and go, and labeling them, if that's helpful to you.

---

* *Visit hayhouse.co.uk/download to download this meditation (see Contents page for further instructions).*

If the sensation that has claimed your attention is pleasant—a delicious sense of looseness in your legs, say, respite from a chronic ache, or a calm, floaty lightness—you may have the urge to grab onto it and make it last. If that starts to happen, relax, open up, and see if you can experience the pleasure without the clinging. Observe the sensation, and allow it to leave when it leaves.

If the sensation arising in your body is unpleasant or painful, you may feel a reflexive urge to push it away. You may feel annoyed by it, or afraid of it; you may feel anxious, or tense. Note any of these reactions, and see if you can come back to your direct experience. What's the actual sensation, separate from your response to it?

If what you sense is a pain, observe it closely. Where do you feel it? In more than one place? How would you describe it? Although at first, pain seems to be monolithic and solid, as we look carefully we see that it's not just one thing. Maybe it's actually moments of twisting, moments of burning, moments of pressure, moments of stabbing. Does the pain grow stronger or weaker as you observe it? Does it break apart, disappear, return intermittently? What happens between twists or stabs? If we're able to detect these separate components of the pain, then we see that it's not permanent and impenetrably solid, but ever-changing; there are spaces of respite between bursts of discomfort.

See if you can zero in on one small detail of it. Rather than take in every sensation that's happening in your back, for example, look at the most intense point of pain. Observe it. See if it changes as you watch it. If it's helpful to you, quietly name those changes. What's actually happening in this moment? Can you see the difference between the painful sensation, and any conditioned responses you're adding to it, such as fighting it, fearfully anticipating future pain, or criticizing yourself for having pain?

If a troubling thought distracts you, let it go. If it's an emotion, focus your attention and interest on its physical properties instead of interpreting or judging it. Where do you feel the emotion in your body? How does it affect or change your body? Whether the physical sensation is pleasurable or painful, continue to observe it directly.

Don't try to stay with painful sensations uninterruptedly for too long. Keep bringing your attention back to the breath. Remember that if something is very challenging, the breath is a place to find relief, like returning to home base.

Allow your attention to move among hearing, following the breath, and the sensations in your body. Mindfulness remains open, relaxed, spacious, and free, no matter what it's looking at. If you feel a physical sensation especially strongly, briefly scan the rest of your body. Are you contracting the muscles around the painful sensation? Are you trying to hold on to a pleasant sensation, bracing your body against its departure? In either case, take a deep breath and relax your body and mind. Pain is tough, but it's going to leave us. Pleasure is wonderful, but it's going to leave us. You can't hang on to pleasure; you can't stop pain from coming; you can be aware. When we practice mindfulness, we don't have to take what's happening and make it better, or try to trade it in for another experience. We just allow the mind to rest on whatever is capturing our attention.

Gently end your meditation. See if you can bring the feeling of being centered within your body, of directly experiencing your ever-changing sensations, into the rest of your day. A few times a day, stop whatever you're doing and become aware of your body. See which sensations predominate. Try to have a direct physical and tactile experience as you're performing everyday activities—feel a water glass against your hand as a cool hardness; when you sweep the floor, sense the exertion in your arms, the tug on the muscles of your back and neck.

EVERYDAY ACTIVITY MEDITATIONS

A friend told me that he'd decided to make brushing his teeth a mindfulness exercise—to slow down and concentrate on each separate step of this usually automatic task. The first thing he noticed, he said, was that he was holding on to the toothbrush so tightly it might have been a jackhammer about to leap out of his hand. He felt this was a useful clue, an indication perhaps that he was using inappropriate force or energy in other activities, from the way he made his bed to the way he held his body as he lay down to sleep.

Often we can take the lessons we learn from observing one single activity and apply them to the rest of our life. See if you can use a part of your everyday routine as a meditation, a time of coming into the moment, paying attention to your actual experience, learning about yourself, deepening your enjoyment of simple pleasures, or perhaps seeing how you could approach a task more skillfully.

Choose a brief daily activity—something you may have done thousands of times but never been totally conscious of. This time bring your full awareness to it; pay attention *on purpose*. Here's a mindfulness exercise you might try:

DRINKING TEA MEDITATION

How many times a day do we perform an action without really being there? When we're simultaneously reading the newspaper, checking our e-mail, having a conversation, listening to the radio, and drinking a cup of tea, where is the taste of that tea? In this exercise we try to be more fully present with every component of a single activity—drinking a cup of tea.

Put aside all distractions, and pour a cup of tea. Perhaps you'll want to make brewing the tea a meditative ritual. Slowly fill the kettle, listening to the changing tone of the water as the level rises, the bubbling as it boils, the hissing of steam, and the whistle of the pot. Slowly measure loose tea into a strainer and place it in the pot, and inhale the fragrant vapor as it steeps. Feel the heft of the pot and the smooth receptivity of the cup.

Continue the meditation as you reach for the cup. Observe its color and shape, and the way its color changes the color of the tea within it. Put your hands around the cup and feel its warmth. As you lift it, feel the gentle exertion in your hand and forearm. Hear the tea faintly slosh as you lift the cup. Inhale the scented steam; experience the smoothness of the cup on your lip, the light mist on your face, the warmth or slight scald of the first sip on your lips and tongue. Taste the tea; what layers of flavor do you detect? Notice any leaf bits on your tongue, the sensation of swallowing, the warmth

TRY THIS
Do a Task in Slo-mo

Restore your attention, or bring it to a new level, by dramatically slowing down whatever you're doing. If you're eating lunch, feel the sensation of the food on your tongue or the pressure of your teeth as you chew, your holding of a fork or spoon, the movement of your arm as you bring the food to your mouth. These specific components of an action may be invisible as you speed through your day.

Try slowing down when you're washing dishes, bringing your awareness to every part of the process—filling the sink with water, squirting in the detergent, scraping the dishes, immersing them, scrubbing, rinsing, drying. Don't hurry through any of the steps; zero in on the sensory details. See if you can be in the present moment as you wash one item. Do you feel calm? Bored? Notice your emotions as they come and go—impatience, weariness, resentment, contentment. Whatever thoughts or feelings arise, try to meet them with the gentle acknowledgment, *This is what's happening right now, and it's perfectly okay.*

traveling the length of your throat. Feel your breath against the cup creating a tiny cloud of steam. Feel yourself put the cup down. Focus on each separate step in the drinking of tea.

You may notice that many judgments come to mind: *I chose the wrong tea. I drink too much tea. I don't give myself enough time to enjoy tea. I should be paying bills, not sniffing tea. Am I running out of tea?* Note these thoughts, and let them go. Simply return to the direct experience unfolding in the moment. Just now; just drinking tea.

REFLECTIONS ON WEEK TWO

Some people who try the walking meditation for the first time don't feel their feet until they look down. The exercise eases us into greater connection with physical sensations as they're happening—so we don't become like the thoroughly disconnected Mr. Duffy in James Joyce's short story "A Painful Case," who "lived at a little distance from his body." Walking in this slow, contemplative way gives us a fresh, immediate experience of our bodies—not a rumor of our feet, or what we remember about our feet, but what our feet feel like that very second. This meditation helps us bring mindful movement into our daily lives.

The Body Sensation Meditation offers a way to see the difference between direct experience of our bodies and the habitual, conditioned add-ons we carry with us. It's especially useful in helping us learn to let sensations arise and subside naturally, without clinging, condemning, or disconnecting. Those three conditioned responses can rob us of a good many chances for authentic happiness. How many times has the wonderful moment in front of us been poisoned because we're fretting over its anticipated departure? I think about a new mother who told me she caught herself feeling such wistfulness at how fast her baby was growing up and away from her that she almost didn't see the lovely child in her arms right then. How many times has an attempt to dodge pain made us miss the sweet parts of bittersweet—the chance to grow in response to a challenge, to help others or accept help from others? How many pleasures escape our notice because we think we need big, dramatic sensations to feel alive? Mindfulness can allow us to experience fully the moment in front of us—what Thoreau calls "the bloom of the present"—and to wake up from neutral so we don't miss the small, rich moments that add up to a dimensional life.

The Body Sensation Meditation is also especially helpful in pointing us toward a mindful approach to pain. It trains us to be with a painful experience in the moment, without adding imagined distress and difficulty. If we look closely at it, the pain is bound to change, and that's as true of a headache as it is of a heartache: the discomfort oscillates; there are beats of rest between moments of unpleasantness. When we discover firsthand that pain isn't static, that it's a living, changing system, it doesn't seem as solid or insurmountable as it did at first.

We can't avoid pain—but we can transform our response to it. One of my students used the Body Sensation meditation to deal with intractable chronic pain, eventually diagnosed as Lyme disease. Again and again, she brought her awareness back to what she was experiencing in the moment, the one moment in front of her. She observed her pain, she said, the way the tide of it surged and receded, its location, the routes it traveled, its shape and texture—sometimes pulsing, sometimes radiating, sometimes jagged as lightning bolts. She watched closely to see how her pain, like everything else in the world, changed. And she found moments of respite that were sustaining to her. She didn't get rid of the pain, but, she told me, "I found the space within the pain."

The science is interesting on this point: Researchers are discovering that for some people, meditation can actually diminish the perception of pain. In 2010, British scientists found that longtime meditators seem to handle pain better than the rest of us because their brains are less focused on anticipating it. After using a laser to induce pain in study participants, the scientists then scanned their brains. Experienced meditators showed less activity in the areas of the brain normally turned on when we anticipate pain, and more activity in the region involved in regulating thinking and attention when we feel threatened. "The results of the study confirm how we suspected meditation might affect the brain," explained Dr. Christopher Brown of the University of Manchester, the chief researcher. "Meditation trains the brain to be more present-focused and therefore to spend less time anticipating future negative events."

FAQs

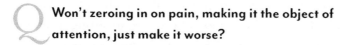

Q **Won't zeroing in on pain, making it the object of attention, just make it worse?**

A Sometimes approaching pain with pinpoint awareness is useful, so that you're feeling it just at its most acute or intense point. At other times it's more useful to step back and be with the pain in a broader way—noticing it fleetingly and then letting it go. What's most important is to approach the pain with a spirit of exploration: For whatever time you're focusing on it, are you open to it, interested in it, paying attention to it? Or are you filled with fear and resentment, drawing conclusions and making judgments about the pain?

Dealing with pain is not a question of endurance, sitting with your teeth gritted and somehow making it through, even if you're feeling great distress at what is happening. Our practice is, as much as possible, to recognize our experience without getting lost in old, routine reactions. The point is to be open not just with pain, but with everything.

Q **I find walking practice much easier than sitting. But is walking "real" meditation?**

A We can practice meditation in four different postures: sitting, standing, walking, and lying down, and each one is equally "real," a complete practice in itself. The obvious difference among them is energy. Meditating lying down will likely generate the least energy, while walking will produce the most. Sometimes people choose to do walking meditation instead of sitting when they're feeling foggy or drowsy. Walking is also a good alternative to sitting when we feel restless and need to channel the extra energy coursing through our bodies. Walking won't disperse that energy but will help direct it so that we experience more balance.

Q When I'm doing walking meditation, it's hard for me not to notice everything going on around me. What should I do?

A There are certainly times when something in the environment draws our attention dramatically. In that case, you might just stop walking and pay full attention to whatever it is for a few moments before letting it go. But if you find yourself stopping every ten seconds because your attention is being snagged by every bird, leaf, or passerby, you might need to shift toward paying more attention to the sensations of movement—not shutting out everything that's happening around you, but not letting your surroundings draw your attention away completely. Aim for a balance.

Q Sometimes when I meditate after work, my body feels tense and twitchy, and I'm distracted. Would I have a better meditation if I did some yoga or other stretches first?

A Knowing this about yourself is a good start. First I'd suggest doing a walking meditation before you sit if you tend to feel restless at the outset. Or you could replace the seated session altogether with a walking meditation if you're in a place where that's possible.

Another option: Right before doing a seated meditation, take five or ten minutes to stretch your body, or do a couple of yoga postures that you know get rid of kinks. Stretch in any way that your body is telling you it needs. Then settle in to your seated posture and begin your meditation session. See if your body has quieted down enough to free you to pay attention to the breath. Of course, if you feel agitation or discomfort while seated, try to be with these feelings in a balanced way to see what you can learn from them.

Q **Sometimes my back and knees really hurt when I sit with my legs crossed—so much that I want to quit. Should I sit in a chair?**

A You could certainly sit in a chair, or you could wait to see whether your back hurts less as you become more familiar with the cross-legged position. You should also check to see if your body is supported and you are sitting in good alignment—do you need cushions under your knees or to add another cushion for height, for example? You might also experiment with seeing what you can learn from the discomfort. Locate it precisely in your body. Be with the sensation for a few moments and watch to see if it changes.

As you observe, it may grow stronger or weaker; it may move around, it may stay the same. Approach it with a spirit of exploration: What am I actually experiencing? Is it totally unpleasant? Is anything about it comfortable? Is it changing? See what you're telling yourself about the pain. *I shouldn't have this pain. I hate this pain. If I still have this pain in half an hour, I won't be able to stand it.* Try to make a quiet mental note of just what you're experiencing in the moment directly, without judging it, adding to it, holding onto it, or pushing it away. Once you've noted the sensation, return your attention to the feeling of the breath. If you find that you're fighting the pain, hating it, it's better to change your posture and begin again. But try seeing what happens when you don't relate to the pain in your usual way and instead observe it with an open mind.

OFF THE CUSHION: EXERCISES FOR PRACTICING MINDFULNESS AND THE BODY

A TIME TO MIND YOUR BODY

Until it becomes second nature, try scheduling an intentional pause for mindfulness to "check in" with your body during a busy day. Set an alarm or write down a promise along the lines of, "Before I transition from *this* to *this*, I will pause." When the moment comes, return to your breath. Then observe any predominant physical sensations—your feet against the floor or your hand holding an object. What do you witness as an actual experience? Take another breath before moving forward in your day.

OUR BODIES IN SPACE

Feel your body in space. I once had a teacher challenge those of us who had come to study with him, "Now touch space." Each one of us picked up our hands and started poking the air with a finger. He laughed and laughed, saying, "You're already touching space. Space is touching you." Sit and feel how space is touching you on all sides. How does it feel?

JOURNAL PROMPT
FOR REFLECTION

~~~~

SUBTLE SENSATION

Bring your attention to your hands. Notice that the direct experience you have is not of "hand," it's of different sensations—pulsing, throbbing, warmth, coolness. You don't have to name these things, but *feel* them. You can also notice that moving into the world of direct sensations brings us to see constant change. Perhaps we would see this as just a hand in the context of "yesterday, today, and tomorrow." But in the realm of "pressure, vibration, warmth, coolness," everything is constantly arising and passing away. Go back and forth between experiencing your hands through a conceptual framework and as a conduit of direct sensation, and write down your experience of each.

THE TAKEAWAY

~~~

For most of us, mindfulness is fleeting. We manage it for a moment, and then we're gone again for a long period of time, preoccupied with the past, the future, our worries; we see the world through the goggles of long-held assumptions. What we're doing in practice is working to shift the ratio, so that we can gather and focus our attention more frequently. Mindfulness isn't difficult; we just need to remember to do it.

One new meditator, a lawyer, said that the walking meditation led him to focus on small physical details he'd previously missed. "I, a noted curmudgeon, find that I'm very grateful for things like a breeze or the sun on the back of my neck. The other day I made it a point to pay attention to the sun and the wind, and how good they felt, as I walked from my office to a meeting that could have been tense. I arrived in a pleasanter frame of mind, more open to hearing the other person's point of view. The meeting went much better than I'd expected. They don't teach sun and wind in law school."

Often people think, *I don't have the right kind of mindfulness, the right level of concentration.* Progress is not about levels; it's about frequency. If we can remember to be mindful, if we can add more moments of mindfulness, that makes all the difference. Countless times a day we lose mindfulness and become lost in reaction or disconnected from what is happening. But the moment we recognize that we've lost mindfulness, we have already regained it; that recognition is its essence. We can begin again.

Mindfulness and Emotions

DEALING WITH THOUGHTS AND FEELINGS

I'VE HEARD SOME WONDERFUL EXPLANATIONS of mindfulness. Sylvia Boorstein, a writer and teacher, calls it "awake attention to what is happening inside and outside so we can respond from a place of wisdom." The Vietnamese Zen teacher and poet Thich Nhat Hanh says, "I like to define mindfulness as the energy that helps us to be there one hundred percent; the energy of our true presence." But my favorite definition comes from a fifth-grader at the Piedmont Avenue Elementary School in Oakland, California.

In 2007, the school launched a pilot program that offered kids five weeks of mindfulness training from a coach who visited classrooms twice a week, leading fifteen-minute sessions on how to have "gentle breaths and still bodies." The students trained their attention by focusing on their breath and noting the emotions that arose. The coach also asked them to cultivate compassion by reflecting—"taking a moment"—before lashing out at someone on the playground. "I was losing at baseball and I was about to throw a bat," one boy told a classmate, according to *The New York Times*. "The mindfulness really helped."

A reporter asked another boy participating in the program to describe mindfulness. "It's not hitting someone in the mouth," the eleven-year-old said.

His answer is wise, wide, and deep. It illustrates one of the most important uses of mindfulness—helping us deal with difficult emotions. It suggests the possibility of finding the gap between a trigger event and our usual conditioned response to it, and of using that pause to collect ourselves and change our response. And it demonstrates in a very real way that we can learn to make better choices.

"He doesn't know what to do with his energy," the student's mother said at a parents' meeting. He was, she explained, usually quick to strike out when he was confused or frustrated. But mindfulness training was changing that pattern. "One day after school he told me, 'I'm taking a moment.'"

This is just what the practice of mindfulness helps us remember. Working with emotions during our meditation sessions sharpens our ability to recognize a feeling just as it begins, not fifteen consequential actions later. We can then go on to develop a more balanced relationship with it—neither letting it overwhelm us so we lash out rashly, nor ignoring it because we're afraid or ashamed of it.

We learn a lot in that middle, mindful place. We begin to discover that, like the Oakland schoolboy, we can always take a moment—to re-center ourselves in our bodies (with a quick body scan, like the one we learned last week, or by following a few breaths), to acknowledge what we're feeling, spot our habitual reactions (whether it's erupting when we're frustrated or silently sulking when we feel we've been criticized), and perhaps decide on a different course of action.

When I first began my meditative practice I was only eighteen, and although I knew I was deeply unhappy, I wasn't aware of the separate strands of grief, anger, and fear roiling inside me. All I felt was a single, seemingly solid bank of sadness. Then, through meditation, I began to look within more clearly, and to detect the various components of my sorrow. What I saw unsettled me so much that I marched up to my teacher, S. N. Goenka, and said accusingly, "I never used to be an angry person before I began meditating!" Of course I was hugely angry; my mother had died, I barely knew my father, I barely knew myself. Meditation had allowed me to unpack that distress. When I blamed him, Mr. Goenka simply laughed—then reminded me of the tools I now had to deal with the difficult feelings I used to keep hidden (more from myself than from others). I could begin to forge a different relationship with my emotions—to find the middle place between denying them and giving over to them—because I had acknowledged them.

I'd taken the first of four crucial steps in dealing with emotions mindfully: to **recognize** what I was feeling. You can't figure out how to deal with an emotion until you acknowledge that you're experiencing it.

The second step is **acceptance.** We tend to resist or deny certain feelings, particularly if they're unpleasant. But in our meditation practice, we're open to whatever emotion arises. If you're experiencing anger, that's what you use as a vehicle for mindfulness; if you're experiencing boredom, use that. We don't blame ourselves if a troubling emotion comes up. And we remind ourselves that emotions arise whether we bid them to or not; we don't have the power to declare, "I've suffered enough. No more grief!" or "Those feelings of betrayal from the divorce? Totally over, never to return."

The third step is to **investigate** the emotion. Instead of running away from it, we move closer, observing it with an unbiased interest. In order to do that we need to take a moment, not only to refrain from our usual reaction, but also to unhook from the object of the feeling. Our usual reaction when we're caught up in a strong emotion is to fixate on its trigger or target, saying to ourselves: *I'm so mad at so-and-so that I'm going to tell everyone what he did and destroy him* rather than examining the emotion itself. When we're neither pushing away from a negative situation nor wallowing in it, we can respond with a new form of intelligence rather than with the same old knee-jerk reaction. Often it's not a matter of solving problems; sometimes a problem dissolves when you shift your relationship to it in a particular way.

Not long after we had opened our Insight Meditation Society retreat center, one of my teachers from India, a man named Anagarika Munindra, came to visit. At the time I was once again feeling waves of anger coming up during my meditation practice. When I told Munindra-Ji that this was distressing to me, he said, "Imagine that a spaceship lands on the front lawn, and some Martians get out and come up to you and ask, 'What is anger?' That's how you should be with your anger. Not 'it's reprehensible!' or 'it's terrifying,' or 'it's justified' but simply 'What is this thing we call anger? What is this feeling?'"

As we observe our anger or study any strong emotion, noticing where we feel it in the body, we're likely to find that it's not one thing but a composite. Anger includes moments of sadness, moments of helplessness, moments of frustration, moments of fear. What seems so solid and unyielding, so inflexible and permanent, is actually moving and changing. (I've noted this before, but we can never be reminded enough.) When we notice this, we begin to feel that strong or painful emotion is more manageable than we imagined.

Acceptance leads to the fourth step—**not identifying** with the emotion. The embarrassment or disappointment you're feeling today isn't your whole résumé, the final word on who you are and who you're going to be. Instead of confusing a temporary state with your total self, you come to see that your emotions arise, last a while, then disappear. You feel some fear, and then you don't. You're resentful, and then you aren't.

The four steps in dealing with an emotion mindfully—recognition, acceptance, investigation, and nonidentification (some teachers of meditation like to use the acronym RAIN)—can also be applied to thoughts. We tend to identify with our thoughts in a way we don't identify with our bodies. When we're feeling blue and thinking lots of sorrowful thoughts, we say to ourselves, *I am a sad person.* But if we bang our funny bone, we don't usually say to ourselves, *I am a sore elbow.* Most of the time, we think we are our thoughts. We forget, or have never noticed, that there's an aspect of our mind that's *watching* these thoughts arise and pass away. The point of mindfulness is to get in touch with that witnessing capacity. Sometimes I ask students to imagine each thought as a visitor knocking at the door of their house. The thoughts don't live there; you can greet them, acknowledge them, and watch them go.

Mindfulness practice isn't meant to eliminate thinking but rather to help us know what we're thinking when we're thinking it, just as we want to know what we're feeling when we're feeling it.

Mindfulness allows us to watch our thoughts, see how one thought leads to the next, decide if we're heading down an unhealthy path, and, if so, let go and change directions. It allows us to see that who we are is much more than a fearful or envious or angry thought. We can rest in the awareness of the thought, in the compassion we extend to ourselves if the thought makes us uncomfortable, and in the balance and good sense we summon as we decide whether and how to act on the thought.

THE FIVE OBSTACLES

Throughout history, wise observers of human behavior have pinpointed over and over again a core group of unhealthy human tendencies that are obstacles to happiness. They're the states of mind that distract us in meditation practice, and trip us up in the rest of our lives. Broadly speaking, they are: desire, aversion, sloth, restlessness, and doubt. And they manifest in a variety of ways—many of which you'll recognize. Desire includes grasping, clinging, wanting, or attachment. Aversion can appear as hatred, anger, fear, or impatience. Sloth is not just laziness, but also numbing out, switching off, disconnecting, and the sluggishness that comes with denial or feeling overwhelmed: *This is going to be diffi-cult; I think I'll take a nap.* Restlessness shows itself as anxiety, worry, fretfulness, or agitation. The kind of doubt we're talk-ing about is not healthy questioning but rather the inability to make a decision or commitment. Doubt keeps us feeling stuck; we don't know what to do next. Doubt undermines wholehearted involvement (in relationships, in our medita-tion practice) and robs us of in-depth experience.

I like to share with students a true story that Sylvia Boorstein tells to illustrate how these five obstacles operate in our lives. A woman she knows left her apartment one morn-ing, headed for work. When she got to her car, parked on the street, she saw, to her shock, that all four tires had been stolen. Her immediate response was to march off to the near-est shopping center and buy a pair of silk pajamas as a way to comfort herself. Only then could she go back home and call the police. This is a perfect example of the mind state of desire in action: The woman couldn't cope with the reality of her situation until she'd fortified herself by satisfying a material want.

Boorstein then goes on to imagine how people influenced by the other hindrances might react to the same situation. A person who tends toward aversion—anger— might discover that the tires have been stolen, get furious, kick the car, and then berate the neighbors for not noticing the theft.

The slothful person just can't cope with having her tires stolen. She goes back up to the apartment, calls in sick to work, and then takes to her bed for the day.

The person prone to anxiety learns of the stolen tires and goes into a downward spiral. *Today, it's the tires,* she thinks, *tomorrow, it will be the car; then after that, it will be me.*

The person prone to doubt launches into a litany of second-guessing—and blame: "Why do I always make such poor choices? Why did I park there? Why do I live here? This must be all my fault." He feels confused and uncertain and is unable to take action that would remedy the situation.

We could call this the tale of Greedy, Grumpy, Slothful, Anxious, and Doubtful. Sometimes we may feel as if we're struggling with all five of these obstacles at once. But however many hindrances arise in the mind, we needn't blame or judge ourselves. Mindfulness practice teaches us how to spot them, and shows us that they're simply passing mind states.

When we acknowledge them, we can decide how, or whether, to act on them.

In general, when hindrances come up in our lives, we're so keyed in to the content, the story, that we don't pay attention to what the state itself feels like. We get hung up, for example, on the object of our desire: *I really want this car. Should I get this upholstery or that upholstery? What about the sound system? It's pricey, but I really love it. How can I swing the payments? I've got to have it!*—instead of turning our attention to the most important question: "What does it feel like to want something so much?" The practice of mindfulness is to take the state itself—in this case, the feeling of desire—as the object of meditation. Can you feel that leaning-forward acquisitiveness, the vulnerability, the unease, the insecurity that is part of grasping, trying to hold on? Can you just be with those feelings and not get involved in the story?

NUTS AND BOLTS

In Week Three, add a fifth day of practice, with a session of at least twenty minutes. Incorporate into your practice one of the Mindfulness Meditations on Thoughts or Emotions learned this week.

PRACTICE PREVIEW

This week we're going to practice being with emotions and thoughts, even intense or difficult ones, in an open, allowing, and accepting way. For many of us, that's the opposite of our default mode—pushing away uncomfortable feelings out of fear or annoyance and doing everything we can to endlessly extend pleasant experiences.

We're also going to continue last week's mindfulness practice—distinguishing what's actually happening in the moment from the add-ons we bring to it, such as shame, projecting into the future, or weaving an entire negative self-image from a scrap of fleeting emotion. Any of these habitual reactions piles extra burdens onto the stress that accompanies a painful situation. My friend lost his job recently, which was difficult and scary enough, but on top of that he transformed a worldwide economic downturn into proof positive that he just couldn't do anything right. Mindfulness meditation helped him become aware of the story he was telling himself: *It's my fault I was downsized; everything is always my fault.* Once he noticed this add-on and examined it closely, he could begin to poke holes in what had seemed like rock-solid logic. Only then was he able to summon the confidence to look for a new job. In our practice, we try to become conscious of these add-ons and see if we can let them go. We cultivate mindfulness to help us distinguish the actual experience from the story we tell ourselves.

In mindfulness meditation, you observe what you're feeling with interest, curiosity, and compassion, then let it go, without beating yourself up over it *(I'm a horrible person!)* or clinging to it *(How can I make this peaceful feeling stay?)*; without musing on its meaning, or coming up with a game plan (though you can do both of those things later, after your meditation session). Mindfulness meditation doesn't eliminate difficult feelings or prolong pleasant ones, but it helps us accept them as passing and impermanent. Our goal is not to hang on to them, nor to vanquish them, but to pay attention to them in a deeper, fuller way.

At first when we work with emotions, we may notice only the obvious ones, the big operatic feelings: anger, grief, joy, fear. As our meditation practice continues, we notice subtler mixes: impatience, infatuation, numbing out, regret, yearning, tenderness. Using the four steps of recognition, acceptance, investigation, and nonidentification, we can experience these nuanced emotions without drowning in them. Mindfulness practice widens our comfort zone, which helps us develop the capacity to be with whatever arises.

MEDITATION ON EMOTIONS*

In this meditation, the state of awareness we're going for is balanced—tranquil and gentle, but also alert and awake, connected to what's going on inside. Recall the way you feel when you hit your stride running or get into a groove swimming, dancing, or chopping veggies for a great meal.

Take a comfortable meditative posture, sitting or lying

* *Visit hayhouse.co.uk/download to download this meditation (see Contents page for further instructions).*

down. Close your eyes, or if you prefer, lower your gaze. Settle into awareness of your body. Do the head-to-toe scan we learned last week if that helps you feel centered. Be aware of sounds as they're arising, then turn your attention to the breath. If you like, use the mental note *in, out,* or *rising, falling.*

Observe the feeling tone in your mind. Does your mind feel calm and peaceful? Are you agitated? Bored? Is there happiness, is there sadness, is your mind in neutral? See if you can open up to and recognize the emotional background as you're with the breath.

As you follow your breath, be aware of any predominant emotions. If any feeling is strong enough to take your attention away from your breath, make it the object of your meditation. Name it, using mental noting if you like. Usually we note two or three times, depending on the strength or duration of the feeling—*happiness, happiness; disappointment, disappointment; boredom, boredom.* (For more on mental noting, see the box on page 126.) See if you can locate the emotion in your body: What physical sensations accompany it? Do you have butterflies in your stomach or a racing pulse? Are your eyelids heavy, your shoulders drawn up? (If no emotions arise that are strong enough to distract you, just keep following your breath.)

Be with the emotion in a soft and relaxed way. Here's one way to tell whether you're doing that: Listen to the tone of your mental noting. If it's harsh or tense—*Jealousy, jealousy! Again!*—make an effort to note more gently. Another useful approach: When you've located the emotion in your body—if, for example, you find that anxiety has created a knot in your stomach—check the rest of your body to see whether some other part is tensing up. Are your shoulders, say, hunching up in reaction to the original response? Consciously relaxing that reactive tension will help you more calmly observe the original object, the knot of tension in your stomach. It may then begin to relax on its own. The very act of observation can sometimes dissipate stress, because we're not buying into the emotion, we're simply watching it. We're not struggling against the experience but taking an interest in whatever feeling arrives and passes away.

If observing your emotions starts to feel overwhelming, return to following the breath, your old friend. Do so at any time during the meditation if you need steadying.

If you're distracted by physical pain, note the emotion generated by it. A twinge or ache might be accompanied by a flash of impatience, irritation, or panic. Observe the emotion, name it, and allow it to leave. Return to following your breath.

If you find you're adding on judgment *(I'm crazy to feel this way!)*, condemnation, or projection into the future, remind yourself that it's okay to be feeling whatever it is that has come up. Try letting go of those reactions as best you can, and coming back to your direct experience in the moment: *What am I feeling right now? What's its nature? Where am I experiencing it in my body?*

Return to following your breath. After a few moments, end the meditation and open your eyes.

During the day, see if you can tune into your emotional landscape, and notice the variety of your feelings.

MEDITATION ON
CALLING UP DIFFICULT EMOTIONS*

Sit comfortably or lie down, with your eyes closed or open. Center your attention on the feeling of the breath, wherever it's easiest for you—just normal, natural breath. If it helps, use the mental note *in, out,* or *rising, falling.*

After a few moments of following your breath, consciously bring to mind a difficult or troubling feeling or situation from the recent or distant past, a scenario that holds intense emotion for you—sadness, fear, shame, or anger. Take a moment to recall fully the situation. Doing that isn't likely to feel comfortable, but stick with it. At any point, you can return to following your breath for respite.

What bodily sensations accompany the emotions this scenario calls up? See if you can tell where in your body you feel these emotions. When you observe the emotion that's arisen, does your mouth go dry? Are you breathing shallowly? Are you clenching your teeth? Is there a lump in your throat? Whatever is happening in your body, note it. If you can feel the emotion in the body (and we can't always do that), it gives you a concrete way to disengage from the story and observe the emotion's changing nature.

Visit hayhouse.co.uk/download to download this meditation (see Contents page for further instructions).

Bring your focus to the part of the body where those sensations are the strongest. You don't have to do anything about them except be aware of them. Once your attention has moved to the bodily sensations, perhaps say to yourself, *It's okay; whatever it is, it's okay; I can feel this without pushing it away or getting caught up in it.* Stay with the awareness of the feelings in your body and your relationship to them, accepting them,

GENTLE NOTES ON MENTAL NOTING

Mental noting, a way to acknowledge briefly whatever is arising in the present moment, serves two main purposes: First, it establishes a sphere of awareness, a small, calm interior space where we aren't caught up in a thought or feeling, aren't reacting to it, but are able to discern it, name it, and move on. Second, noting provides a kind of instant feedback system: We can see whether we're labeling our experiences with openhearted acceptance (*yep, this is what's happening right now*) or with fretfulness and resentment (*oh, no! not envy again!*). If we hear that tone of judgment or self-criticism, we can let it go and say to ourselves again, more kindly and evenly (*ah, there's envy*). Try to make the noting a warm, open acknowledgment.

Noting performs a third interesting function: As do many aspects of the meditation process, it reminds us vividly and efficiently of the way things continually change. Many thoughts and emotions will come, be noted, and go during the course of our meditation session, some of them very pleasant, some upsetting, some neutral. They arise; they subside. Our job is simply to note them without judgment, to see the truth of this very moment, and then breathe.

letting them be, softening and opening to them. As you sit with them awhile, do the sensations change? How?

Remember that often what we are feeling is not just one emotion; grief may include moments of sorrow, moments of fear, of powerlessness, maybe even moments of relief, anticipation, curiosity. See if you can break down the emotion into its component parts. Notice all the different things you feel. Are

Early in my practice, I let this simple method for dealing with distraction become a distraction itself. I'd sit and think, *Is what I'm feeling pain, or is it discomfort? You couldn't really call it agony, that's way too big a word, but what about anguish?* I was becoming a human thesaurus—and completely losing track of my experience. I soon learned that the word isn't the point; it's just shorthand for recognizing what's arising in the moment and keeping ourselves from becoming swept away in a tide of thought. The note needn't be elaborate; it's simply a quiet act of recognition: *Ah, this is what's happening right now: There's sadness, there's remembering.*

As some of my students have been quick to point out, rather gleefully, mental noting is itself a form of thought. "Aren't we supposed to be working on letting go of thought while we're meditating?" they ask. I answer that noting is certainly a thought, but it's a skillful use of thought; it helps support awareness by stopping us from getting lost in thought, or swept away. Thoughtful noting points us back to the moment and to our breath.

You don't have to use mental noting all the time; often just noticing a thought or feeling is enough. But sometimes mental noting can be a good way of connecting quickly and clearly with your immediate experience.

there any positive mind states mixed in with the mostly negative? Any negative mind states flavoring the positive? Staying with the feeling and untangling the various strands may lead you to realize that what you thought was a thick wall of misery is a constantly shifting combination of emotions. This perception alone makes the feelings more manageable.

You may notice yourself resisting these difficult emotions and the bodily sensations that accompany them—pushing them away and feeling ashamed of them. Or perhaps you find yourself getting pulled into them—replaying an argument, or reliving feelings of rage, helplessness, or humiliation.

Perhaps the emotions that the thought or situation call up are so upsetting that you start to cry. If you do, that's okay; it's part of your experience. You can become aware of how you're relating to the tears—how your body reacts, what blend of emotions accompanies the crying, what stories you tell yourself about crying. Maybe mixed in with your sadness is regret, irritation, or fear that the tears will never stop.

If you feel overwhelmed by emotions, use awareness of your breath to anchor your attention in your body. This helps you return to the present moment. If you find yourself thinking, *I will always feel this way,* or *If only I were stronger/ more patient/smarter/kinder, I wouldn't feel this way,* return to the simple truth of the moment—sitting and being aware of your breath. See if you can recognize that the emotion is a temporary state, not your total self.

And when you are ready, open your eyes. Take a deep breath and relax.

During the day, if a difficult emotion arises, see if you can apply these skills of awareness to it.

MEDITATION ON POSITIVE EMOTIONS*

In order to be resilient enough to face difficulties—for example, a friend who can't be helped or a day full of sudden changes outside of our control—we need to find and nurture the positive parts of ourselves, and make a point of paying attention to experiences that give us pleasure.

Too often we focus on what's wrong with us, or on negative, unpleasant experiences. We need to make a conscious effort to include the positive. This doesn't have to be a phony effort, or one that denies real problems. We just want to pay attention to aspects of our day that we might overlook or ignore. If we stop to notice moments of pleasure—a flower poking up through the sidewalk, a puppy experiencing snow for the first time, a child's hug—we have a resource for more joy. This capacity to notice the positive might be somewhat untrained, but that's okay. We practice meditation for just this kind of training.

Sit or lie down on the floor in a relaxed, comfortable posture. Your eyes can be open or closed.

Now bring to mind a pleasurable experience you had recently, one that carries a positive emotion such as happiness, joy, comfort, contentment, or gratitude. Maybe it was a wonderful meal or a reviving cup of coffee, or time spent with your kids. Perhaps there's something in your life you feel

* Visit hayhouse.co.uk/download to download this meditation (see Contents page for further instructions).

129

especially grateful for—a friend who is always there for you, a pet excited to see you, a gorgeous sunset, a moment of quiet. If you can't think of a positive experience, be aware of giving yourself the gift of time to do this practice now.

Take a moment to cherish whatever image comes to mind with the recollection of the pleasurable experience. See what it feels like to sit with this recollection. Where in your body do you feel sensations arising? What are they? How do they change? Focus your attention on the part of your body where those sensations are the strongest. Stay with the awareness of your bodily sensations and your relationship to them, opening up to them and accepting them.

Now notice what emotions come up as you bring this experience to mind. You may feel moments of excitement, moments of hope, moments of fear, moments of wanting more. Just watch these emotions rise and pass away. All of these states are changing and shifting.

Perhaps you feel some uneasiness about letting yourself feel too good, because you fear bad luck might follow. Perhaps you feel some guilt about not deserving to feel this happiness. In such moments, practice inviting in the feelings of joy or delight, and allowing yourself to make space for them. Acknowledge and fully experience such emotions.

Notice what thoughts may be present as you bring to mind the positive. Do you have a sense of being less confined or less stuck in habits? Or perhaps you find yourself falling back into thoughts about what went wrong in your day, what disappointed you—these thoughts can be more comfortable because they are so familiar. If so, take note of this.

Does the mind try to build stories around the positive or pleasurable experience? Do you tell yourself, for example, *I don't deserve this pleasure until I give up my bad habits,* or *I must find a way to make this last forever?* Try to become aware of such add-on thoughts and see if you can let them go and simply be with the feeling of the moment. No matter what story or add-on arises, come back to your direct experience. Ask yourself, *What sensations are present in my body? What am I feeling right now? What's happening?*

You can end the meditation by simply sitting and being with the breath. You can be with the breath gently, as though you were cradling it. When you're ready, you can open your eyes.

Bring this skill of gentle interest, curiosity, and attention to your encounters throughout the day. Notice pleasurable or positive moments, even those that may be seemingly small.

THINKING MEDITATION

Sit or lie comfortably. You can close your eyes or keep them open, whichever makes you feel most at ease. Feel the space within which you're sitting, touching you from all directions; you don't need to reach out. Feel the ground underneath you. Notice how the earth is supporting you; you don't have to manufacture that—you can trust it.

Let your attention settle on the feeling of the breath. You can notice that the breath is coming and going, according to its own rhythm, filling your body, and leaving, connecting you to the world around you. You can receive it, let it go. It's happening without your needing to control it; you can settle back and allow it.

See what thoughts may be present in your awareness. You might think of them as events in the mind. And when a thought arises that's strong enough to take your attention away from the breath, simply notice it as thinking. You can note it—*thinking, thinking*—no matter the content. Whether it's a lovely thought or an awful one, it's just a thought.

If you're able to, note the thought more distinctly, *planning, remembering, worrying, anticipating*. Don't struggle to find the right word, but if one comes clearly, use it and see what happens as you note the thought. You don't have to judge yourself, you don't have to get lost in the thought or elaborate it; you recognize that it's simply a thought. Very gently let go and bring your attention back to the feeling of the breath.

Some of our thoughts may be tender and caring, some may be very painful or hurtful, but they're all thoughts. Remember the image of thoughts as clouds moving across the sky. Some are very light and fluffy, very inviting. Some are quite ominous and threatening. And you can just let them all float on by. See them, recognize them, let them go, bring your attention back to the feeling of the breath.

Our habitual tendency is to grab on to a thought and build an entire world around it, or push it away and struggle against it. Here we stay even, balanced, calm. We simply recognize *it's a thought; it's not who I really am.* By its very nature a thought, however intense, is impermanent; it is visiting, it is arising due to conditioning or habit. Very gently let it go. Bring your attention back, one breath at a time.

Again feel the space within which you're sitting and how it touches you from all directions. Feel the ground underneath you, supporting you. Notice how the space is touching you, notice how the earth is supporting you. You can feel these things, and you can trust them. Open your eyes and relax.

REFLECTIONS ON WEEK THREE

The practice of mindfulness allows us to see our lives more clearly and honestly. And the clearer our vision—the more firsthand information we have about ourselves and the world—the better able we are to make good decisions, and the less fragmented we feel. "When you look into a pool of water," writes Jon J. Muth in his children's book *Zen Shorts*, distilling ancient wisdom, "if the water is still, you can see the moon reflected. If the water is agitated, the moon is fragmented and scattered. It is harder to see the true moon. Our minds are like that. When our minds are agitated, we cannot see the true world."

You may recognize that the thoughts and emotions that come up in this week's meditations are part of recurring patterns—that you're hearing a lot of what I call old tapes, the familiar, habitual mental soundtrack I mentioned in the introduction. It's helpful to acknowledge these tapes of ours, perhaps even to good-naturedly name them: *Oh, there's the "Everyone Is Wrong but Me"* (or *"Everyone Is Right But Me"!*) *tape; there's the "Drama Queen" tape, the "I'm a Failure" tape, the "You Can't Fight City Hall" tape, the "Why Bother?" tape.* Once we spot them and perhaps name them, we can remind ourselves that these thoughts are just visiting, they're not essentially who we are. We can't stop them from visiting, but we can let them go.

One student who warmed to the idea of naming the patterns that he discovered during mindfulness meditation was a fifty-nine-year-old man, a contractor who'd just gone back to school to become a master gardener. "What you said about tapes really resonated with me," he said. "I realized that I always play what I'd call the 'One False Move' tape. When I did the meditation that included calling to mind a difficult situation, I thought about the last day of my master gardener certification program. I'd killed myself getting everything done—an extensive plant notebook, and a big report on my internship at a local wetlands park where I was supervising the volunteers. The teacher heaped praise on me, but she said I could have organized the work brigades better, and she made some suggestions. And I was miserable. I felt like a total failure. One negative comment had canceled out twenty good things. During the meditation about a difficult situation, as I pictured that day, I realized how familiar that 'one false move and I'm doomed' feeling is. I don't know yet why I play that tape—but at least now I know it happens."

Meditation is like going into an old attic room and turning on the light. In that light we see everything—the beautiful treasures we're grateful to have unearthed; the dusty, neglected corners that inspire us to say, "I'd better clean that up"; the unfortunate relics of the past that we thought we had gotten rid of long ago. We acknowledge them all, with an open, spacious, and loving awareness.

It's never too late to turn on the light. Your ability to break an unhealthy habit or turn off an old tape doesn't depend on how long it's been running; a shift in perspective doesn't depend on how long you've held the old view. When you flip the switch in that attic, it doesn't matter whether it's been dark for ten minutes, ten years, or ten decades. The light still illuminates the room and banishes the murkiness, letting you see things you couldn't see before. It's never too late to take a moment to look.

JUST NON-DO IT

As long as you're taking a moment, take a few more.

The fourth-century Chinese philosopher Chuang Tzu told this story: There was a man so displeased by the sight of his own shadow and footsteps that he determined to get rid of both by running away from them. But every time he put down his foot, there was another step, and his shadow kept up with him without the slightest difficulty. He thought he must not be running fast enough. So he ran faster and faster and faster, without stopping, until he finally dropped dead of exhaustion. He failed to realize that if he merely stepped into the shade, his shadow would vanish, and if he sat down and stayed still, there would be no more footsteps.

Practicing mindfulness meditation is making the choice to be still—to step into the quiet shade instead of running away from difficult thoughts and feelings. We sometimes call meditation non-doing. Instead of being swept away by our usual conditioned reactions, we're quiet and watchful, fully present with what is, touching it deeply, being touched by it, and seeing what is happening in the simplest and most direct fashion possible.

At the Insight Meditation Society, someone once created a mock motto: "It is better to do nothing than to waste your time." I loved it. Doing nothing in this case really means not doing many of the things we usually do, like holding on to or hiding from our experience, so that we can get new perspectives, new insights, and new sources of strength. Sitting quietly and observing mindfully is a particularly productive way of "doing" nothing. The poet Pablo Neruda speaks of this in his poem "Keeping quiet":

> . . . If we were not so single-minded
> about keeping our lives moving,
> and for once could do nothing,
> perhaps a huge silence
> might interrupt this sadness
> of never understanding ourselves
> . . . Perhaps the earth can teach us
> as when everything seems dead
> and later proves to be alive.

FAQs

Q The instruction to follow my breath and return to it if I get distracted seems clear. But when a feeling comes in with a bang, and that becomes the object of the meditation, am I supposed to analyze it?

A When a strong feeling takes you away from your breath, go with it. It would be too much of a struggle to come back to the breath.

Let's say it's envy. If as soon as the envy comes, we start hating it and hating ourselves and trying to push it away, then there's not going to be a lot of learning going on. Similarly if we get lost in the envy and spin scenarios in which the object of our envy rises to greater triumphs while we sink to greater and greater humiliation—no learning. Mindfulness brings us to a place in the middle, where we sit with the question *What is envy?* We don't try to figure it out. Rather, the question is a prod for observing what's happening in the body and the mind. You feel the envy and look at it; you watch your thoughts. That's one reason why some meditative techniques emphasize mental noting—it gives us a more concrete way to say, *Oh, it's envy,* and not get lost in either extreme of holding on or pushing away.

When something has that kind of intensity, you stay with it and make it the object of your meditation. But while you're staying, I suggest coming back to the breath occasionally, even for just a moment or two. One of the functions of the breath is to give you a touchstone and a template: *Oh, right—this is what it feels like just to be with something—plain old inhaling and exhaling—without getting lost in it, without pushing against it.* And then we take that balanced awareness back to the envy—or whatever the "bang" is. It's fine to go back and forth between the two, getting back in balance whenever you need to. No need to analyze; simply observe and experience.

Q While I try to practice fully experiencing whatever is present during a meditation session, how do I know when it's time to let go of observing and acknowledging the feelings or thoughts that have come up and move back to following the breath?

A Sometimes it's hard to clock that moment of letting go, and you just have to go with your intuition and not be anxious about meditating perfectly or absolutely correctly. If you're cultivating awareness, you are doing it right. In terms of specific tools for more fully experiencing what is present, I've found using mental noting to be quite helpful. So, for example, if something comes up, like a large emotion or a cascade of thinking, I'm gently labeling, *joy, joy* or *thinking, thinking,* at a pace that keeps directing my attention toward the experience of what's going on. But if you begin to lose interest in the experience you're observing, or if you feel the balance among thought, feeling, and sensation slipping because you're starting to resent what's happening or getting too drawn in, those are good signs to let go and see if you can return your attention to the feeling of the breath.

Q During meditation, old feelings of fear and self-doubt came up. Even though I opened to them and confronted them, the effects lingered; I continued to feel very down and doubtful. What's the best way to deal with that?

A You may not think so at the time, but the very fact that fear and self-doubt are arising is a good thing. You get a chance to learn to relate to them differently, to practice not identifying with them but instead observing them with compassionate curiosity.

Opening to these feelings is not just biding time, or making do until somehow you can figure out some other way to make them leave. The less you cling to the feelings or identify with them—*Oh, this is really me. The fifty generous impulses I had today don't count; I'm really a doubting, fearful person*—the more likely they are to be dispelled. But everything rests on your relationship to the experience: How are you going to be with these feelings?

My colleague Joseph Goldstein has a suggestion for this sort of thing: When you're having a really difficult time, imagine that the thoughts coming up in your mind are coming up in the mind of the person sitting next to you. It's quite interesting. When the thoughts arise in our own minds, we have a very complex set of reactions: We can't believe this is happening to us; we thought we'd gotten rid of those feelings long ago; we can't figure out what to do about them. But when we imagine the thoughts arising in the person sitting next to us, we think, *Oh, you poor guy! That must really hurt. May you be happy.*

So the question is: How are you going to relinquish your attachment to, your identification with, this emotion? It will likely come back—these things tend to be very deeply rooted. But it doesn't matter how many times it comes back, because you have the means to work with it skillfully.

Q Can meditation help with depression?

A Depression has many causes. While it is important to investigate its possible biochemical basis and explore psychotherapeutic help, meditation might also be beneficial.

In a landmark Oxford University study led by John D. Teasdale, the cofounder of Mindfulness-Based Cognitive Therapy (MBCT), one group of people suffering from recurring depression went through eight weeks of mindfulness training, while another similar group received traditional cognitive therapy. Thirty-seven percent of the people in the group treated with MBCT, which teaches patients to look at their thoughts nonjudgmentally as events in the mind, experienced a relapse, compared to 66 percent of those in the traditional-therapy control group.

Many meditators report that they benefited from exercises showing them that their depression is actually made up of many strands—anger, loss, and guilt among them. Even though painful feelings may arise as you separate out these various strands, once you see that depression consists of many changing states and not one unchanging and overwhelming state, it becomes more manageable. And the compassion you develop in meditation enables you to regard whatever you discover within yourself, even if painful, with greater kindness. For a more in-depth discussion of compassion toward the self and others, see Week Four. If your depression is persistent or severe, I would strongly encourage you to work with a qualified meditation teacher, and to seek other professional help.

Q **Sometimes it's recommended that we just stay with whatever feeling arises, and other times I hear that we can change those feelings by walking in nature or relaxation exercises, etc. It's confusing.**

A The primary approach of mindfulness is to pay attention to what's happening and to develop a different relationship to our experience so that we're not rejecting it or hating it, but we're also not overwhelmed by it. So mindfulness has an inherent sense of balance. But the reality is that there are times when mindfulness is not that easy. We may be exhausted, or we may not be able to find balance through coming back to the breath, or mental noting, or other techniques we employ, or our mindfulness may be too intermittent. So there are a whole host of approaches to help us come back into balance and once again be mindful. It's fine to explore these methods instead of following a traditional mindfulness practice. Sometimes people think, "Oh, I blew it, I can't do the real thing." But it's not like that at all. Get up and take a walk, go out into nature, do some stretches, or whatever it might be, if it brings you enough calm or perspective to reenter a place where you can relate differently to what arises in your experience.

Q **I can't seem to shake this uncomfortable notion that things are never going to get better, so I either give up and fall asleep in meditation or get so wound up that I just want to run away. How can I use meditation without having it make things worse?**

A You already see the add-ons: You had a crummy feeling and projected it into the future, judged yourself for it, and felt ashamed and afraid. That is a tremendous insight. The more aware you can be in that way, the more you can see that the crummy feeling is a construct, and that it's already in the process of changing—it's not fixed and permanent. When you watch that process in your meditation practice, even though what you're looking at feels bad, it's ultimately very liberating. I would suggest doing a walking meditation rather than sitting right now, because part of what you're describing is a low energy state. Walking would help rev up and channel your energy. But even if you choose to sit, investigating your "tormented" state will pick up your energy. Investigating it doesn't mean asking "Where did this come from, and is it biological?" but rather, "What is this feeling? What's happening?" Just watching the feeling as it unfolds in your session is the first step in beginning to move through it. Mindfulness teaches us that "the best way out is always through," as Robert Frost wrote. See if you can expand the moment of awareness to include everything that's happening, even if you don't know where it's going to lead. It may not seem so right now, but you need to trust that this kind of compassionate observation eventually leads to new understanding.

Q **If I stay in the moment, how do I plan for the future? If I accept whatever thought or feeling comes up, how do I keep from being totally passive?**

A Some people fear that if they develop the capacity for mindfulness, if they become proficient in the practice of meditation, everything in their lives will become a dull gray blob. They think mindfulness might lead to just looking at life rather than being actively involved in life

This is not so. Mindfulness brings us closer and closer to the natural properties of any moment, any experience— what it looks and feels like without any of our add-ons. This doesn't mean we lose our ability to differentiate between what we like and what we don't. But we do come to understand how much our own worldview affects what we make of each experience, and how the same experience might be interpreted very differently by another person. We still react to things—but consciously, knowing what we're doing when we're doing it.

And being mindful of the moment doesn't mean that we give up savoring memories or setting goals. I like to quote Thich Nhat Hanh: "To dwell in the here and now does not mean you never think about the past or responsibly plan for the future," he says. "The idea is simply not to allow yourself to get lost in regrets about the past or worries about the future. If you are firmly grounded in the present moment, the past can be an object of inquiry, the object of your mindfulness and concentration. You can attain many insights by looking into the past. But you are still grounded in the present moment."

The more directly and intimately we connect with our thoughts, feelings, and experiences, the more powerfully proactive we become—because we can make informed, better choices, and not just be driven by unexamined habit. Mindfully accepting a negative feeling, such as rage or envy, doesn't mean that you've given yourself carte blanche to wallow in a negative emotion or act on it irresponsibly. Quite the opposite. Until you can acknowledge a thought or emotion as part of your human repertoire—observe it to see that it isn't permanent, isn't all you are—you can't create a healthy relationship to it.

OFF THE CUSHION: EXERCISES FOR PRACTICING MINDFULNESS AND EMOTIONS

MINDING THE GAP

Becoming mindful of our emotions and habitual responses helps us not be overwhelmed by the uncertainties of daily life. Let's explore this relationship in action for a day. As you eat, work, run errands, and care for yourself and loved ones, try to identify waves of strong emotions. What does the monologue in your head begin to say about—or add on to—the actual experience in response? Can you pause and create some space around the emotion, allowing it to arise and pass away? As the day continues, are there patterns you witness? Which need further exploration? When the day closes, note observations in your meditation journal.

THE RE-BALANCING ACT

This point in our program is a good time to ponder your values. Maybe cultivating relationships is of great value to you, but distractions habitually pull you toward technology or keep you at your desk. Maybe you value a deep connection to your spiritual practice, work, health, or education, but self-judgments have hindered you from taking steps towards satisfying growth. Ponder the values that make you feel strong, joyful, and inspired. Consider these as you continue your meditation practice. You are cultivating the attention we all need to best nurture what we really care about.

JOURNAL PROMPT
FOR REFLECTION

MAKING IT RAIN

Let's apply the RAIN technique detailed on page 114–117 to one strong emotion you felt today. First, RECOGNIZE the emotion by pinpointing it as fear, sadness, frustration, joy, excitement, and so on, and write it down. Next, look at the emotion you've chosen and ACCEPT it as one of the many temporary, complex emotions felt by all humans. Now, INVESTIGATE it: Are there other emotions embedded within it? Lastly, can you attempt NON-IDENTIFICATION of that original emotion? The emotion is a temporary, conditioned experience. It does not ultimately define you.

THE TAKEAWAY

This week, we worked on recognizing that painful feelings (anger, fear, hopelessness, envy, resentment, frustration) and uncomfortable thoughts (*I hate everyone! I'd like to walk out the door and keep going! I wish he'd just disappear! Why isn't*

this bad thing happening to her, not me?) are a rich and undeniable part of human experience, and that they're beyond
our control, as are all thoughts and feelings. We reminded
ourselves that thoughts aren't the same as actions. We continued to observe our habitual responses and judgments that
get between us and direct experience. Unacknowledged, they
drive our behavior without our consent. If we change the way
we approach emotions while we're meditating, we can eventually bring those healthy changes into the rest of our lives.

Like the boy who refrained from punching someone in
the mouth, we practiced creating some space between our
emotions and our habitual responses to them. Just staying in
the moment is a triumph to savor. If we're busy running away
from our immediate experience, or are submerged in it and
defined by it, we aren't going to learn much. If we forge a new
relationship with our experiences, we have a new understanding of ourselves and, ultimately, of others.

Here are three stories from students who, in various ways,
changed their relationship with an experience. They were
able to apply to their lives the skills—being with emotions,
staying in the moment, and recognizing their add-ons—that
they had learned in meditation practice. They were, in short,
able to take a moment and choose a different response.

One beginning meditator, a speech therapist, was
amazed when her meditation practice helped her catch herself adding long-held, unexamined assumptions to a difficult
situation. "I was sitting, following my breath on the morning
of an interview for a great job in a very enlightened school

district," she says. "It was the perfect job for me. The thought that kept popping up was *I won't get it. I won't get it.* I can't believe how often I told myself that during the session; it's a wonder I got any breathing done.

"After my twenty minutes of sitting was up, I had a talk with myself. I poked at the assumption that I wouldn't get the job by sort of presenting the evidence: *You've had a job ever since college, so you can get jobs. Yeah, but not really good jobs like this one. Your jobs have been fine. Anyway, someone has to get this one; it might as well be me. I'm certainly qualified.* Then I heard myself telling myself, *You're mighty pleased with yourself, aren't you, missy?* in a voice that I recognized as my mom's, definitely. The important lesson for me was that I wouldn't have noticed the way I have of shooting myself in the foot—by talking myself out of feeling confident, and in my mom's voice—if I hadn't sat quietly, and breathed, and observed my thoughts in a slow, quiet way. Maybe someday I'll stop being mayor of Worst-Case-Scenario Town. This was a good first step."

Another woman used her practice to change a negative scenario. "I was part of the team proposing a big marketing campaign for the electronics company where I work," she says. "I did a long, complicated preliminary report for my new boss, and she sent it back to me for major revisions. I was furious. I started thinking about every unreasonable boss I'd ever had, and how hard I'd worked, and how she'd probably hate everything I ever turned in, or maybe we'd never agree and I'd be fired, and then what would I do—but then I figured I'd better make the changes she asked for and turn the thing back in. I did—and she sent it back for more changes. I got even madder and spent even more time thinking about past grievances and my miserable future. I fumed over how unfair and unbearable the situation was. But then I thought, *wait— that's an assumption. I can test it; that's what I've been practicing. Is it really unbearable? Is it really unfair? If I take away the imagined future, and the history that belongs to another boss and an entirely different set of circumstances, is the present really so awful?*

"And then I decided to follow my breath, the way I was learning to do, let go of my anger, and just be there with the stupid report. I said to myself, *If you put aside your injured pride and your anxiety about what the new boss thinks of you, are you suffering right this minute?* And I had to say that I wasn't. *Have the boss's comments been helpful?* The answer was yes. *Is this project interesting?* Yes again. I saw that if I stayed in the moment and just focused on the work—and let go of my reactions to all the other stuff—this was a really interesting challenge. I calmed down and dived in. My boss actually returned the report one more time, but I wasn't upset. She said she was impressed by the finished product, and especially by my attitude."

Recently, a woman told me a story that illustrates, as she put it, "the power of meditation by proxy." It highlights two very common experiences—dealing with the feeling of boredom, and adding on an unhappy future. "A friend of mine joined Weight Watchers, and she told me she's struggling," the woman reported. "I was very sympathetic—I'd been there, and done that. But then she said something that really caught my ear, something I wouldn't have noticed before I took a meditation class. She was complaining about how boring the program was, and she said, 'And if it's boring after two weeks, imagine how boring it's going to be after two months!' *Textbook case!* I thought, and said, 'Why are you worried about how bored you're going to be in two months? All you have to think about is right now, today. Just this afternoon, as a matter of fact. In two months you'll either be so thrilled with your new body you won't care what you're eating, or you'll have quit, or something else will have happened that you can't even predict. And if you're feeling bored, get to know your boredom. Make friends with it! Really examine it. See what the boredom feels like in your body.' At that point my friend looked so . . . unreceptive, let's say, that I said, 'And load up on blueberries; they're great and a cup is only one Weight Watchers point!' I hope she'll come around; I'll talk to her about all this again in a few weeks. I'm just excited at the way these concepts from meditating seem to have sunk in for me."

Even during the relatively brief duration of our meditation session, we can see that our thoughts, feelings, and physical sensations, no matter how powerful, arrive, depart, and alter kaleidoscopically. Accepting (if only for a moment) the fact of impermanence and continual change is acknowledging a big truth in a small way. Learning to feel comfortable with our thoughts and feelings as they change is the first step in being more comfortable with life as it is, not as we wish it would be. Mindfulness helps us make friends with the idea that nothing is permanent—not joy, not sorrow, not tedium.

And seeing that our thoughts and emotions change so often, we no longer have to think, *if I feel jealous, I must be a terrible husband and a bad person.* We realize that we're a person who has that thought, among many. When we know our thoughts, we neither dodge them nor get lost in them. Instead, we can decide when and if we should act on them; we can better discern which actions will lead to happiness and which to suffering. Meditation allows us to see and accept ourselves as we are in the moment—sometimes hot-tempered and sometimes mellow, sometimes cowardly and sometimes strong, sometimes ashamed and sometimes proud, sometimes confused and sometimes clear. It allows us to understand that the way we're feeling right now isn't the way we're always going to feel, and it isn't the whole of who we are.

Lovingkindness

CULTIVATING COMPASSION
AND TRUE HAPPINESS

WHEN I RAN INTO RACHEL, a friend and one of my meditation students, she surprised me with her enthusiastic greeting. "I've fallen in love with my dry cleaner!" she said.

The last time I'd seen her was six months earlier, at a retreat I'd taught on the power of lovingkindness. Seeing that I looked elated at her confession (knowing her dating history), she laughed. "No, I haven't fallen in love with him romantically. My dry cleaner was one of the people I picked to be the focus of my lovingkindness meditation."

I'd asked retreat participants to choose someone in their lives they didn't have strong feelings about, someone, in fact, they barely noticed, and to begin regularly paying attention to that person during meditation sessions, picturing them and wishing them well. "Now," Rachel said, "every day when I meditate I hold this man in my heart and consciously wish him well. I find that I'm eager to go into the store to see him. I really care about him."

While this man was no doubt a perfectly fine dry cleaner, Rachel wasn't feeling suddenly connected to him out of gratitude for his stain-removing skills. She wasn't indebted to him; she hadn't learned of his particular sorrows or tribulations. The change in their relationship came about simply because she was continually including him in her field of attention instead of overlooking him.

Again and again I hear responses like Rachel's from people doing lovingkindness meditation—the practice of paying attention to ourselves and others with a sense of interest and care. During lovingkindness meditation, we focus caring attention first on ourselves, then on someone we know well, on a neutral person, like Rachel's dry cleaner, and on a series of others. Students tell me that when they try this practice, they feel a strong new sense of connection, not only to people who were once nearly invisible to them—I saw one woman's face light up when she discussed a teller at her bank, a virtual stranger who'd become the unwitting recipient of her warm wishes—but to people they know but had dismissed, dissed, or distanced themselves from. "I started doing lovingkindness meditation and aiming good wishes toward a coworker who is particularly hard to deal with," one man told me. "I was very, very skeptical. The guy didn't get any less difficult, but instead of just being exasperated, I felt more compassionate toward him. I started to see that he had his struggles, just like all of us."

Sometimes lovingkindness is described as extending friendship to ourselves and others—not in the sense of liking everyone, or dispensing universal approval, but more as an inner knowing that our lives are all inextricably connected. Lovingkindness is a power of the heart that honors this connection. When we practice it, we acknowledge that every one of us shares the same wish to be happy, and the same vulnerability to change and suffering.

In the movie *Dan in Real Life,* starring Steve Carell as a single dad, there's a line that seems to sum up the nature of lovingkindness. One of the characters says, straight from the heart, "Love is not a feeling, it's an ability." I gasped loudly in the theater when I heard it.

Lovingkindness is a form of love that truly is an ability, and, as research scientists have shown, it can be learned. It is the ability to take some risks with our awareness—to look at ourselves and others with kindness instead of reflexive criticism; to include in our concern those to whom we normally pay no attention; to care for ourselves unconditionally instead of thinking, "I will love myself as long as I never make a mistake." It is the ability to gather our attention and really listen to others, even those we've written off as not worth our time. It is the ability to see the humanity in people we don't know and the pain in people we find difficult.

Lovingkindness isn't the same as passion or romantic love, and it's not sappy sentimentality. As I've said, we don't necessarily like or approve of everyone to whom we offer lovingkindness. Focusing our attention on inclusion and caring creates powerful connections that challenge the idea of an "us/them" world by offering a way to see everyone as "us."

Here's one way that works on a small scale. Several performers have told me that they do the following brief lovingkindness meditation if they have stage fright: Standing in front of an audience, before they start acting, playing music, or reciting a poem, they send out wishes for the well-being of everyone in the room. "When I do that," one singer told me, "I no longer have a sense of the audience as a group of hostile people out there waiting to judge me. I feel, okay, here we all are together."

Sometimes lovingkindness comes in the form of compassion, the stirring of the heart in response to pain or suffering—our own, or that of others. Compassion overcomes the tendency to isolate ourselves if we're the ones in pain, or to avoid others whose pain we fear will discomfit us. When I toured a wing of Walter Reed Army Hospital before spending an afternoon offering a meditation class to nurses working there, the woman giving me the tour said, "You know, the nurses who can stay here are not the ones who get lost in the suffering; they're the ones who can connect to the resiliency of the human spirit." For these nurses, compassion doesn't mean being so overcome with sorrow that they can't help their patients. Rather, by tapping into their own resiliency and that of their patients, they're motivated to act.

Sometimes lovingkindness comes in the form of sympathetic joy, the ability to rejoice in the good fortune and happiness of others. When something really good happens and people are genuinely happy for us, their response feels like a tremendous gift. Some people may have a harder time summoning sympathetic joy at our success; they may smile on the outside, but we sense they'd be happier if we weren't quite so happy. The ability to feel sympathetic joy helps us ignore that inner voice we sometimes hear when learning of a friend's triumph, the voice that says, *Oooh, I'd feel better if he had a little less going for him right now.*

Because it helps us feel connected to others, lovingkindness meditation deepens our ability to feel sympathetic joy. When we can go beyond feeling threatened or diminished by the success of another, we come to understand that it takes nothing away from us. In fact, it increases our own chances for happiness. The Dalai Lama points out that there are so many other people in this world, it simply makes sense to make their happiness equivalent to our own because then, he says, our chances of delight "are enhanced six billion to one. Those are very good odds."

Robert Thurman, professor of Buddhist studies at Columbia University, often uses an amusing and powerful image to describe what living compassionately, with lovingkindness, could look like: "Imagine you're on the New York City subway," he begins, "and these extraterrestrials come and zap the subway car so that all of you in it are going to be together . . . forever." What do we do? If someone is hungry, we feed them. If someone is freaking out, we try to calm them down. We might not like everybody, or approve of them—but we're going to be together forever, so we need to get along, take care of one another, and acknowledge that our lives are linked. Isn't living on planet Earth like being in that subway car? We're all together forever; our lives are linked.

This week we're going to practice meditations that allow us to extend lovingkindness, compassion, and sympathetic joy to everyone on our subway car, including ourselves.

One way to nourish lovingkindness is to look for the good in someone. Looking for the good doesn't mean we ignore the bad, or that we condone behavior that we consider unhealthy or dangerous. But if we fixate only on what's wrong with a person, we'll naturally feel more and more estranged. Maybe we can

TRY THIS
Enough Happiness to Go Around

Sometimes when I'm having a hard time feeling sympathetic joy for another person's good fortune, I ask myself the question: *What would I gain from this person's not getting such and such?* And it is quite clear to me that I don't benefit at all from someone else's loss.

Often, without consciously realizing it, we're convinced that the good thing someone else got was destined for us but got detoured to them by some hideous, unjust twist of fate. But, of course, we need to look at that assumption.

Cultivating sympathetic joy opens the door to realizing that the happiness of others doesn't take anything away from us. In fact, the more joy and success there is in the world, the better it is for everyone.

glimpse only a tiny sliver of good. But if we can focus on that small piece of goodness in our dealings with that person, then we won't have to reach across such a wide divide of us-versus-them.

That happened to me when I first practiced lovingkindness. I was working with a teacher in Burma who told me, "I want you to go back to your room and think of somebody and think of the good in them. And then go through other categories of people, like someone you hardly know and someone you have difficulty with, and think of the good in them." My first thought was, *I'm not going to do that. That's what stupid people do—go around looking for the good in everybody. I don't even like people who do that!* But I was in a traditional Burmese monastery, and when your teacher suggests you do something, you don't say, "I don't feel like it." So I did it. And the lovingkindness worked in just the way it's supposed to. Picturing a man whose behavior I generally found irritating and ungenerous, I remembered a time when I saw him be particularly kind to a friend in great physical pain, and in an unassuming way, so that she didn't feel pitied or condescended to. *Uh-oh* I thought, when the memory surfaced. *That complicates things. It's hard now to think of him as permanently,* only *bad.*

But it complicated things in the right way: I didn't deny the difficult, or pretend it wasn't there, but I no longer rigidly categorized that man as totally one way. As a result, I felt less distance between us. When I allowed myself to look for the good, I felt connected to people in a different way.

That's the key to practicing lovingkindness—recognizing that all human beings want to be part of something fulfilling or meaningful; that we're all vulnerable to change and loss; that our lives can turn on a dime—in an instant we could lose a loved one, our life savings, a job. We go up, and we go down, all of us. Vulnerability in the face of constant change is what we share, whatever our present condition. Fully understanding this, we can respond from the heart. Lovingkindness meditation allows us to use our own pain and the pain of others as a vehicle for connection rather than isolation. Maybe when people are acting unskillfully we can look beyond their actions and recognize that they're suffering, and that they, too, want to be happy.

PRACTICE PREVIEW

The practice of lovingkindness meditation is done by silently repeating certain phrases that express kind wishes first for ourselves, then for a series of others. The customary phrases are usually variations on *May I Be Safe* (or *May I Be Free from Danger*), *May I Be Happy, May I Be Healthy, May I Live with Ease*—may daily life not be a struggle. The "May I" is not meant to be begging or beseeching but is said in the spirit of generously blessing ourselves and others: *May I Be Happy. May You Be Happy.*

You don't have to try to manufacture a certain emotion as you engage in this meditation; you don't have to pretend you like people you don't. You can send people lovingkindness without liking them. You're acknowledging your connection.

The power of the practice is in gathering all our attention, all our energy behind each phrase.

One of my students told me that at first the whole idea of lovingkindness meditation seemed hokey and rote to her, but she focused on the phrases nevertheless. Despite her doubts, she felt something stirring and opening within her, a deepening and widening of compassion as she sent good wishes to herself and into the world. "At first nothing seemed to be happening," she said. "Then I goofed something up, I forgot a parents' meeting at my kid's school. And instead of feeling mortified and giving myself hell, which is what I usually would have done, I said to myself, *Poor old thing—you've got too much on your mind.* That really startled me—and made me think differently about lovingkindness meditation. I guess I wasn't just going through the motions after all. Before I would have seen only my mistake, but because of lovingkindness meditation, I was open to seeing the good and cutting myself some slack."

Like that woman, many of us have a tendency to focus on what we don't like about ourselves. These thoughts aren't always inaccurate, but through force of habit we can be very one-sided in our perceptions, overlooking a lot of what's positive. Maybe we criticize ourselves for not doing something perfectly, when in fact it was actually good enough. Or we recall how tough the afternoon was and forget the delight of the morning. Life's draining enough; this skewed view of ourselves depletes us so that we have an even harder time nourishing ourselves. The first exercise will help us have a more balanced and compassionate view.

NUTS AND BOLTS

In Week Four, add a sixth day of practice, with a session of at least twenty minutes. Incorporate one or more lovingkindness meditations into your week.

CORE MEDITATION: LOVINGKINDNESS*

Sit or lie down comfortably on your back. Your eyes can be closed or open. Begin by offering lovingkindness to yourself by saying silently, *May I Be Safe, May I Be Happy, May I Be Healthy, May I Live with Ease.* Repeat the phrases inwardly with enough space between them so that they're pleasing to you. Gather all of your attention behind one phrase at a time.

If you find your attention wandering, don't worry. You can simply let go of distractions and begin again. *May I Be Safe, May I Be Happy, May I Be Healthy, May I Live with Ease.* Feelings, thoughts, or memories may come and go; allow them to arise and pass away. Here the anchor is not your breath but the repetition of these traditional phrases. *May I Be Safe, May I Be Happy, May I Be Healthy, May I Live with Ease.*

Call to mind a benefactor, someone who's helped you—a person you know who's been good and kind to you,

---

Visit hayhouse.co.uk/download to download this meditation (see Contents page for further instructions).

or someone you've never met who's inspired you. Picture the person, say her name to yourself, get a feeling of her presence, and offer the phrases of lovingkindness to her. Wish her what you've wished for yourself: *May You Be Safe, May You Be Happy, May You Be Healthy, May You Live with Ease.* Thoughts may arise when you're picturing your benefactor. You might say to yourself, *Why does this person, who is so great, even need my good wishes?* Just let the thought pass away as your attention steadies on the repetition of the phrases.

Even if the words of the phrases don't totally fit, even if they feel strange or awkward, no matter; they're the vehicle for connection. *May You Be Safe, May You Be Happy, May You Be Healthy, May You Live with Ease.*

Call to mind someone you know who's hurting or having a difficult time right now. Picture him, say his name to yourself, get a feeling of his presence, and offer the phrases of lovingkindness to him. *May You Be Safe, May You Be Happy, May You Be Healthy, May You Live with Ease.*

If you find your attention wandering, you needn't be discouraged; just gently let go, and come back, one phrase at a time.

Call to mind someone you might encounter now and then—a neighbor, a checkout person at the supermarket, someone you see when you walk your dog. Perhaps you don't even know his name. But picture him, get a feeling of his presence. Though you don't know his story, you can know that he wants to be happy just as you do, that he's vulnerable to pain or loss just as you are. And you can wish him well. *May*

You Be Safe, May You Be Happy, May You Be Healthy, May You Live with Ease.

Call to mind a difficult person, someone you have trouble getting along with, or whose words or actions are difficult for you (see sidebar, pages 164–165). If you pick a difficult person but find that sending her lovingkindness is too hard, then just go back to sending lovingkindness to yourself. In that moment, *you're* the one who is suffering, so you're quite worthy of some compassionate attention.

Finally you can offer your well-wishes, the force of lovingkindness, to all beings everywhere, all people, all creatures, all those in existence, known and unknown, near and far. *May All Beings Be Safe, May All Beings Be Happy, May All Beings Be Healthy, May All Beings Live with Ease.*

And when you feel ready, you can open your eyes. See if you can bring lovingkindness into your day, finding a few opportunities for silent repetition of these phrases for yourself and for the people around you.

LOVINGKINDNESS MEDITATION FOR TIMES OF EMOTIONAL OR PHYSICAL PAIN

Our intuitive wisdom often tells us to let go, to be peaceful, to relinquish efforts to control. But our cultural conditioning and personal history tell us we should hold on to people, pleasure, and distractions in order to be happy.

continued on page 166

NOTES ON LOVINGKINDNESS
FOR A DIFFICULT PERSON

When you resolve to send lovingkindness to a difficult person, don't start with the most hated person in your life or on the world stage. Instead, choose someone mildly troublesome—perhaps someone you're a little afraid of or with whom you're in a bit of conflict.

We start with someone relatively manageable because we need to be able to observe our reactions without being overwhelmed by them. We do the practice not with a heavy heart, but as an exploration that allows us to look gently at ourselves and see all our various resistances: the ways we hold back our compassionate attention and refuse to let go of our set ideas about the person in question.

You might find yourself feeling angry at the person who is meant to be the recipient of your lovingkindness. Sometimes anger can bring clarity: it can cut through social niceties, denial, collusion, and pretense. But often anger leads to delusion. We get caught in a very narrow definition of who we are, who this other person is, what any of us might become, and we forget that change is possible. If you find yourself feeling angry, try to recall the limitations you've previously experienced in this state and how these limitations have made you miss the bigger picture.

People often confuse letting go of anger with letting go of principles, values, and a sense of right and wrong. But that's not what needs to happen. We can maintain the clarity of our views without getting lost in anger's toxic aspects: fixation, lack of options, loss of perspective, destructive and damaging actions, and forgetting what we care about most. This is the dawning of the strength of compassion.

Lovingkindness for a difficult person is about seeing what happens when we recognize a connection with someone instead of focusing only on our feelings of conflict; when we pay attention to that person's suffering and not just his or her transgressions.

As you become more comfortable with the practice, you're likely to find you can do it with some ease of heart, and perhaps you can even extend lovingkindness to someone who has hurt you more powerfully.

The phrases you use to send lovingkindness to a difficult person might have to be crafted carefully so that you don't feel a tremendous struggle. You can try out your own versions of the following:

May you be filled with lovingkindness.

May you have happiness and the causes of happiness,
such as clarity and kindness.

May you be free of suffering and the causes of suffering,
such as ill will and envy.

May you be free of anger, enmity, and bitterness.

Sending lovingkindness to a difficult person is a process of relaxing the heart and freeing yourself from fear and corrosive resentment— a profound, challenging, and liberating process, and one that takes the time it takes. Someone once asked, in response to impatience and frustration at not being able to offer full-hearted lovingkindness, "Whose timeline are we working on?" Of course, we aren't working on anyone's timeline but our own.

continued from page 163

Often we find ourselves in a struggle between our own wisdom and our conditioning about clinging and control. An especially important time to heed our intuition is when we're challenged by emotional or physical pain.

This meditation may help you do that. Use one, two, or even three of the lovingkindness phrases below. Alter them in any way you like, or create new phrases that have personal significance.

First try this practice for five to ten minutes. Then move on to a Breathing Meditation (from Week One, page 48), or the Lovingkindness Practice that begins on page 161. If you find that sadness, distress, fear, or discomfort continue to divert your attention, go back to experimenting with the phrases in response to your pain.

Start by sitting or lying on the floor comfortably and take a few deep, soft breaths to let your body settle. Bring your attention to your breath, and begin to say silently your chosen phrases in rhythm with the breath. Or simply settle your attention on the phrases themselves. Feel the meaning of what you are saying, but don't try to force any particular emotional response. Let the practice carry you along.

> *May I accept this pain without thinking it makes me bad or wrong.*
> *May I remember that my consciousness is much vaster than this body.*
> *May all those who have helped me be safe, be happy, be peaceful.*

May all beings everywhere be safe, be happy, be peaceful.
May my love for myself and others flow without limit.
May the power of lovingkindness support me.
May I be open to the unknown, like a bird flying free.
May I accept my anger, fear, and worry, knowing that my
*   heart is not limited by them.*
May I be free of danger, may I be peaceful.
May I be free from anger, fear, and regret.
May I live and die in ease.

When you feel ready, open your eyes.

LOVINGKINDNESS MEDITATION FOR CAREGIVERS

When I led a retreat for caregivers at the Insight Meditation Society, there were mothers and fathers; sons, daughters, and spouses; nurses and hospice workers; therapists, chaplains, medics, and many more. What was striking to me, besides their evident fatigue, was how many of them regarded their service, however difficult or frustrating, as a privilege. It was a beautiful testament to their hearts. I also realized that for anyone in a continuing caregiving role, with all the best will and good-heartedness in the world, burnout is the specter that hovers close.

Skillful caregiving depends on balance—the balance between love and compassion for oneself and love and compassion for another; the balance between opening one's heart fully and accepting the limits of what one can change. Moving our hearts toward balance allows us to care and yet still cope because of that caring.

Some years ago, at the request of Roshi Joan Halifax, who founded a training program in contemplative end-of-life care, I wrote a lovingkindness meditation especially for caregivers, in honor of their incredible work and in the hope of giving them support. This is an adaptation of that meditation.

The phrases we use reflect the balance we seek. Choose one or two phrases that are personally meaningful to you. Some options are offered below. You can alter them in any way you like, or create others that have personal significance.

To begin the practice, sit or lie down comfortably. Take a few deep, soft breaths to let your body settle. Bring your attention to your breath, and begin silently to say your chosen phrases over and over again, in rhythm with the breath. You can also experiment with restricting your attention to the phrases, without using the anchor of the breath. Feel the meaning of what you are saying and let the practice carry you along.

> *May I find the inner resources to be able to give to others*
> *and receive myself.*
> *May I remain peaceful, and let go of expectations.*
> *May I offer love, knowing I can't control the course of life,*
> *suffering, or death.*
> *I care about your pain, yet cannot control it.*
> *I wish you happiness and peace, and know I cannot make*
> *your choices for you.*

*May I see my limits compassionately, just as I view the
limitations of others.*

*May I see you as I wish to be seen, as big as life itself, so
much more than your need or your pain.*

When you feel ready, open your eyes.

MEDITATION ON
SEEING THE GOOD WITHIN*

Sit or lie in a relaxed, comfortable posture. Your eyes can
be open or closed. First, see if you can think of one good
thing you did yesterday. It needn't be big or grand. Maybe
you smiled at somebody; maybe you listened to them. Maybe
you were starting to get annoyed at a slow shop clerk, but you
let go of your irritation. Maybe you took out your recycling,
emailed an interesting article to your uncle, thanked a bus
driver. Now think of two more things.

Remember that it's not conceited or arrogant to consider what you've done right. It's quite replenishing to delight
in the good that moves through us. For a few moments, sit
with the recollection of what you did right.

If at this moment you can't think of something good you
did, that's okay: Sitting down to do this exercise, to meditate,
counts. It's a way of befriending ourselves, of being willing to

---

Visit hayhouse.co.uk/download to download this meditation (see Contents page for further instructions).

expand our awareness, to step out of some ruts and try something new—and that's very positive.

Now picture a benefactor, someone who's helped you; think about the good within them. Appreciate their efforts and acts of kindness.

Think of a good friend. Picture the kindnesses they've performed, and the meaningful times you've had together. Appreciate the good within them.

Think of someone you know who's having a difficult time right now. Think of the times they've reached out to help others, their own sources of strength. You can see that this person is not just their problem, but something bigger.

Think of a difficult time in your own day. Can you see yourself as being bigger than your problem, with a potential for growth and change? Remembering that something like a crammed schedule or an upset spouse will change, or that if you lose your temper or feel overwhelmed, you can begin again is "being bigger than the problem."

Think of someone you have a bit of difficulty with, a conflict. See if you can find some good in things they've done, choices they've made. If not, simply recall that like all beings, they want to be happy.

Close with a few moments of reflection on the fact that all beings want to be happy—you, your friends, the person who's giving you trouble. *All beings want to be happy, may they be happy.* You can silently repeat those phrases again and again. *All beings want to be happy, may they be happy.*

When you're ready, end the meditation.

After this exercise, did you get a glimmer that there might be more room to get a fuller perspective on things? That bigger sense of space is equanimity, balance. Having equanimity doesn't mean that we never get overwhelmed or exhausted; it means we work with our attention to remind ourselves of our options. When we are having a rough time, we remember that this isn't the whole picture of who we are. When we're having an ordinary day, we remember that we have a resource that allows us to be generous to ourselves and acknowledge our connection to the human community.

MEDITATION ON QUIETING THE INNER CRITIC*

This meditation can be done in any posture, eyes open or closed; just be relaxed. Call to mind a difficult emotion you've felt recently—jealousy, fear, greed. And notice how you feel about that emotion. Are you ashamed of it? Do you dislike yourself for it? Do you feel you should have been able to prevent it from arising? Do you consider yourself in some way bad or wrong for having this feeling? Now see what happens if you change the word "bad" to "painful." See if you can recognize that the jealous or fearful feeling is a painful state, a state of suffering. See what happens to your relationship to that feeling as you make this change.

*Visit hayhouse.co.uk/download to download this meditation (see Contents page for further instructions).

171

Now see what that emotion feels like in your body, once you begin to hold it with some kindness and compassion. Observe the various sensations; the pain is there and the compassion is there surrounding it. Notice the effect if that sense of "bad" or "wrong" comes back. When you catch yourself being harshly critical and replace that habit with compassion for yourself, you are practicing lovingkindness.

And you can reflect again on the fact that you aren't able to prevent negative feelings from arising. You don't need to be overcome by them, defined by them, to act on them or feel ashamed if you have them. This is just in the nature of things, for ourselves and for others. We can commit ourselves to trying to see them more quickly, to recognize their painful nature, to have compassion for ourselves, and to let go. We can commit ourselves to remembering that when someone else is acting badly, whatever negative emotion is motivating them also puts them in a painful state, and we can have compassion for them.

And when you feel ready, end this meditation.

LOVINGKINDNESS WHILE WALKING

You can add lovingkindness practice to the walking meditation introduced in Week Two. But rather than focusing on the sensations of movement, we focus on the silent repetition of lovingkindness phrases.

Start by repeating two or three phrases for yourself—for example, *May I Be Peaceful. May I Be Happy. May I Be Safe.* As you walk, some of your attention will rest on the repetition of these phrases, and some will rest on your surroundings. As someone comes into your consciousness—a person walks by; you hear a dog bark or a bird call; or you have a vivid memory of someone—you quickly include them with a phrase: *May You Be Happy*. And then you come back to resting your attention on the phrase for yourself. When your attention wanders, just start over, repeating, *May I Be Peaceful. May I Be Happy. May I Be Safe.*

The return to the phrases for oneself gives us a steady object of concentration, though we're free to recognize and include all those who come strongly into our awareness. *May I Be Happy. May I Be Peaceful. May I Be Safe. May You Be Happy, May You Be Peaceful, May You Be Safe.*

Maybe the image comes to mind of someone we envy, or of someone we're a little afraid of. As we're walking, we can send them lovingkindness: *May You Be Happy. May You Be Peaceful. May You Be Safe.*

And when you feel ready, you can bring the exercise to a close.

CIRCLE OF LOVINGKINDNESS MEDITATION

Imagine yourself sitting in the center of a circle made up of the most loving beings you've ever met. Or perhaps you've never met them but you've been inspired by them. Maybe they exist now or they've existed historically or even mythically. That's the circle. And there you are in the center of it. It's a circle of love. You can experience yourself as receiving the energy, the attention, the care, the regard, of all of these beings. Silently repeat whatever phrases are expressive of what you would most wish for yourself, not just for today, but always. Phrases that are big, that are open. You can use the traditional phrases we've been using, or you can choose phrases that are personally meaningful to you, such as *May I Be Peaceful* or *May I Be Free of Suffering*. Choose three or four phrases.

Then imagine everyone in the circle surrounding you sending you these phrases of lovingkindness. All kinds of different emotions may arise. You might feel gratitude and awe. You might feel shy, and wish you could disappear and have everyone in the circle send lovingkindness to one another and forget about you. You might feel quite unworthy of the attention, and undeserving of the care. You might feel fabulous. Whatever emotion may arise, try to just let it pass through you. Your touchstone is those phrases that have meaning for you. Imagine your skin is porous, and you're receiving this energy. You don't need to do anything special to deserve this kind of acknowledgment or care; it comes simply because you exist. And you can allow that quality of compassion and love to flow right back out toward that circle, and then toward all beings everywhere, so you can transform what you receive into giving.

When you feel ready, you can open your eyes, and relax.

REFLECTIONS ON WEEK FOUR

It may seem odd to aim your caring attention to billions of beings (and by the way, you're not expected to love every single being by the end of Week Four). But ending the exercises with well-wishes for all reminds us that we're connected to a vast network of lives and that small daily shifts in behavior and intention can radiate outward exponentially.

You can vary the traditional phrases and make them your own—*May I Feel Ease of Heart,* for example. They need to be general enough so that they can be offered to those whom you know and those whom you don't know. (So *may I get season tickets to the Steelers* isn't really appropriate.) I heard about a spontaneously created phrase that I found deeply moving. When my friend's daughter Willa, then seven, heard about the London subway bombing in July 2005, she was deeply saddened. Her eyes filled with tears and she said, "Mom, we should say a prayer." As she and her mother held hands, Willa asked to go first. Her mother was stunned to hear Willa begin with, "May the bad guys remember the love in their hearts."

You may find, as you continue with lovingkindness practice, that it transforms you in ways you weren't quite expecting. Mindfulness meditation, which we learned in Weeks Two and Three, enables us to see the distinction between our actual experience and the story we're weaving from it—our add-ons—and allows us to choose whether to pursue that story or not. Lovingkindness meditation has the power to change our story: If our most ready story, the first response that shapes how we see ourselves and our world, is one of isolation, alienation, or fear, it can become one of connection, caring, and kindness.

Some common negative narratives that lovingkindness can rewrite:

I'm worthless. When we extend lovingkindness to ourselves—through reminding ourselves of what we do right in the Meditation on Seeing the Good and the well-wishes we send to ourselves in the Lovingkindness Meditation—we begin to poke holes in that old, painful story. Making a point of acknowledging positive emotions and accomplishments, as we do in this practice, gives us a truer picture of ourselves and a greater sense of being sustained and nourished.

I'm alone. Acknowledging our interconnectedness begins to erase the sense of isolation.

If someone else is happy, that means less happiness for me. As we develop the capacity for sympathetic joy, we begin to understand that there's plenty to go around.

Only certain people count. When we practice lovingkindness meditation, we experiment with opening our attention to include those whom we might have overlooked or have objectified because we see them as a function (the hotel maid, the UPS guy) rather than as a person, and we learn to value everyone.

Recently I was able to use lovingkindness to transform the story I was telling myself. I thought specifically about Robert Thurman's scenario of the zapped subway car when I found myself stuck in an airplane sitting on a runway for four and a half hours. It was sweltering; people started yelling "let me off this plane!"; the pilot got on the PA and sternly told them they couldn't. I wasn't very cheerful myself. I was going to teach in Tucson, and I couldn't get in touch with the people who were picking me up; I was concerned about them. I was hot, and I felt pounded by the people shouting around me. Then I remembered Dr. Thurman's teaching example. I looked around the cabin, and thought, *Maybe this is my subway car, and these are my people.* And in fact my perception changed with my attitude; I felt much more interest in and concern for the people around me than I did resentment. I stopped adding to the cloud of ill will in the plane. Did it help, in some small way? It helped me shift the narrative. It showed me that if we remember we're interconnected, we remember that what each of us does matters.

FAQs

Q **Can doing lovingkindness meditation actually change how we feel about a difficult person?**

A I once received a call from a doctoral student who had interviewed fifteen or sixteen people about their lovingkindness practice. She said every one of them had told her the same thing: In the course of doing the practice, they'd had the insight that whenever someone acts badly, they're coming from a place of pain. I found this interesting, because the practice isn't necessarily directed toward having that insight. We're not asked to reflect on that, or ponder it; it's not offered as something you have to undertake as a belief. But everybody she'd spoken to for her research experienced the same change in their feelings. When we alter the way we pay attention, we get a very different sense of the intricacies of someone else's life. We also understand much more clearly that we ourselves are coming from a place of pain when we act recklessly or unskillfully, and we can extend that observation to others.

Q Sometimes the pain of others awakens compassion in my heart; sometimes I think their troubles are their own fault. Am I a terrible human being?

A You're a human being. Recognizing pain doesn't always lead to compassion. We might be frightened or repulsed by the sight of someone's pain and decide to look the other way. We might blame them for their troubles, believing that they need to make more effort and just get it together already. Our compassion may be blocked because we blame ourselves for being ineffectual in a world that needs so much help, or because we feel guilty about something we did or said (or didn't, but feel we should have). Maybe we ourselves are in pain and feel we don't have enough energy to be compassionate toward someone else. Any of these things might block compassion.

Compassion is truthful: It's acknowledging with equanimity that this is what's going on. In the cases you're talking about, it might mean acknowledging that yes, this person is getting in his own way; he's not handling his troubles very skillfully. But compassion ultimately involves seeing difficult states like fear, greed, and jealousy not as bad and wrong and terrible but as states of suffering. The more we do that, the more compassion will spontaneously arise within us.

Q **If you send lovingkindness to someone but don't feel any emotion toward the person, does that mean the practice isn't working?**

A In my experience, there are many times when we do lovingkindness practice and there's no feeling—but that doesn't mean nothing is happening. The love we're contemplating is recognition of a connection that's actually deeper than emotion. The phrase is really the bottom line, because it's the expression of our intention to connect, to include rather than exclude, to pay attention in a different way. We gather our intention behind the phrase and hold it lightly. We don't try to wrest feeling out of it. You have to let the practice carry you. Sometimes the words may not carry emotion for you, but they're working in subtle ways nonetheless. Maybe your expectation of what you think you're supposed to feel—a surge of sentimental love accompanied by chirping birds—is getting in the way of your seeing the subtler, more profound changes occurring slowly within you.

Q **Sometimes I can include the whole world in my lovingkindness meditation—except a couple of people I'm really mad at. What should I do when I come up against that feeling?**

A The Dalai Lama said, "If you have an enemy and you think about them all the time—their faults and what they've done, and your grievances—then you can't really enjoy anything. You can't eat; you can't get a good night's sleep. Why give them that satisfaction?" It's common sense: The more absorbed we are in another person's state of mind, the more obsessed by them, the less free we are. So it's often out of compassion for *ourselves* that we practice lovingkindness—which may not necessarily mean liking these people but can mean developing a different perspective about them. You can start with remembering that all of us want to be happy—including people who aren't doing a very skillful job of it.

Q I'm afraid I'm losing the ability to defend or look out for myself. With all this openhearted lovingkindness in me, I feel like I'm wearing a sign that says "Do with me what you will. I accept you."

A This is a very important question. Through our experience with lovingkindness, we will come to see that compassion doesn't necessarily leave us weak or sentimental or susceptible to being used by others. But until we discover that, of course we worry: "I'm so openhearted. I'll just smile and let anybody do whatever they want to me or to other people." That's our conditioning; we're likely to have grown up hearing "give 'em an inch and they'll take a mile" or even "everybody's out to get you."

We have this idea that if we're coming from a compassionate place, we can only be nice and say yes to everything. But sometimes the most compassionate response might be saying no—refusing to enable someone's destructive behavior, setting a limit, or trying to the best of your ability to keep someone from hurting himself. Practicing lovingkindness doesn't mean that you're no longer discerning or proactive.

A friend of mine is a wonderfully empathic therapist. One day a man came to see her, beseeching her to take him on as a patient. She found his political views alienating, his feelings about women repugnant, and his behavior quite annoying. In short, she didn't like him at all and urged him to find another therapist. But he very much wanted to work with her, so she finally gave in and took him on.

Once he became her client, she tried to look at his unskillful behavior with compassion instead of with contempt and fear. She began to see all the ways in which his life was very difficult, all the ways he had shut himself off from others. Soon, even though she continued to see his behavior as undeniably unpleasant, she found herself feeling that she needed to be his ally, to help him find the way out of his suffering. Even though I don't believe she ever liked him, or approved of most of his views, she came to care deeply about him.

Q **I'm in a very competitive profession, and I have difficulty rejoicing in the success of others. And then I hate myself for being so ungenerous. How can I deal with those feelings?**

A The painful feelings you describe are rooted in the belief that the other person's success and your misery are permanent states, rather than simply life's unfolding. Joy for others can be tough, and what makes it tough is our assumption that there isn't enough good stuff to go around, so that someone else's fortune means less available for us; that the good fortune meant for us somehow got rerouted and went to someone else instead. In the moment when you have those feelings of envy or resentment, the point isn't to say, "I'm a horrible person because I'm jealous," but to observe what your habitual reaction is—and to see that it's making you suffer.

Your response to spotting your add-ons can be a very gentle relinquishing—*I don't need to go there. I've been there, I can let that go*—or, depending on where the roots of your greatest resentment lie, a knowledge that this too will change. It's really about drawing on wisdom that we all possess and saying, "Okay, everything changes. I'm going to move on."

One way to cultivate greater sympathetic joy is to connect with happiness in our own life. When we believe we have nothing, it's almost impossible to take pleasure in the happiness of others. Like any kind of generosity of the spirit, joy for others depends on a feeling of inner abundance that's distinct from how much one has materially or objectively in this world. The knowledge that our lives are worth something releases our capacity to care about others and rejoice in their success. Lovingkindness meditation helps us tap into that knowledge.

Q Is it invasive to wish someone well if they don't seem to be open to receiving it?

A I wouldn't hesitate to send lovingkindness to that person. This isn't a program for improvement: *May you be happy by getting a new personality.* It's a heartfelt wish that is freely given, with no strings attached. And it can be received, or not received, or received in a strange way, or received a long time after it's been offered. All of that is a mystery. But if you're attached to a specific result—*May you be happy tonight in the following fifteen ways*—then you need to do some letting go. When we're doing lovingkindness practice, it's easy to fall into having expectations about the results, maybe thinking to ourselves, *I've been doing lovingkindness meditation for you for a month. Why aren't you happier?* But we have no control over what happens after we focus our caring attention.

When someone seems to be perpetuating his own suffering by his choices, decisions, and actions, we can be sad or condemn ourselves because we could not make him change—or we can have the courage to keep offering the wish that he be free of his suffering, without feeling we should be able to change his behavior. This is where a sense of equanimity comes in—a kind of underlying peace and spacious stillness of mind that allows us not to be overcome or upset when something doesn't work out as we would like. Equanimity is a balance that allows us to say, yes, this is how things are, without weakening our love or compassion.

OFF THE CUSHION:
EXERCISES FOR PRACTICING
LOVINGKINDNESS

~~~~~

YOUR SUBWAY CAR

Oftentimes, patterns in our lives have us returning to a "crowded subway car"—a public place that triggers negative emotions toward our fellow human beings. Let's anticipate the next time we enter such a space. Where in your commute, workday, familial responsibilities, or elsewhere do you often feel anger or impatience towards strangers? Envision entering that space and silently extending lovingkindness to all within it. How does this change how you feel here? Apply this practice the next time you find yourself approaching this space.

PREDICT YOUR GOOD

Ponder an upcoming social event, job situation, or intimidating activity. Are you already rehearsing potential negative outcomes? Let's change that. Write a note of appreciation to yourself, such as *I worked really hard on this presentation* or *I was nervous to try this class but showed up anyway.* Tuck the note where you'll see it shortly after the event so you can pull it out and see what happens when you include a positive perspective.

JOURNAL PROMPT
FOR REFLECTION

~~~

A CIRCLE OF COMPASSION

Struggling to cultivate self-compassion? Write out a current painful or challenging situation, detailing your experiences and emotions. Now, picture a trusted loved one sitting next to you. Imagine they are describing this scenario to you as if it was theirs. How do you respond? Write down what you imagine your reaction to be. Now compare how you speak to this friend and how you have been speaking to yourself in facing this challenge. If you've been harsh, try responding to yourself as you would to your friend. What's it like to speak kindly to yourself?

THE TAKEAWAY

~~~

Lovingkindness meditation practice doesn't require pretending to feel things you don't; it's not about forcing yourself to like everyone. It's really an experiment in attention, in being more fully present with ourselves and others, in being willing to step out of the rut of habit and look at ourselves and others in a different way. If we're in the habit of seeing only the negative in ourselves and missing the positive, we can experiment with turning our attention to the goodness within us. If we're in the habit of ignoring the humanity of strangers or people we don't know well, we can experiment with being open and aware, taking an interest, connecting. If we're in the habit of not really listening while conversing, we can experiment with being more fully present with the next person we speak to. If we're in the habit of classifying and dismissing people based on what we think we know about them, we can experiment with listening with fresh ears, giving our full attention. If we're wholehearted, open, interested, we may find that people surprise us.

Another experiment centered on the power of loving-kindness meditation. In 2008, researchers at the University of Wisconsin found that lovingkindness meditation actually changes the way the brain works. In their study, a group of novice meditators and and a group of longtime meditators engaged in a lovingkindness meditation. First they visualized a loved one and sent him or her well-wishes; then they sent such wishes to all beings, and finally they entered a resting state. The researchers used fMRI to observe the brain functions of the two groups of meditators, and they compared them with those of a nonmeditating control group. While they meditated, participants were repeatedly exposed to sounds that were positive (a baby laughing, for example), negative (the cries of a baby in distress or a person in pain), or neutral (restaurant background noise). The nonmeditating control group heard the same sounds. Brain scans showed that in both novices and experts, but not in the control group, the sounds activated areas of the brain known to be connected to empathy—and that the experts experienced more empathy when exposed to negative sounds during lovingkindness meditation than did the novices. The researchers also found that both meditating groups showed greater thickening of the insular cortex, a part of the brain associated with regulating emotions, and more activity in the amygdala, the part of the brain that assesses the emotional content of incoming stimuli, than did the non-meditating control group. The investigators concluded that the practice of lovingkindness meditation trains the brain to make us more empathic and more capable of reading subtle emotional states.

Lovingkindness meditation dispels the illusion of an *us* and a *them*, there is only us. We can take that vision of life into everyday encounters and situations. Today doesn't exist apart from the network of relationships and influences that brought us to this moment in our lives. How many people were involved in some way in your decision to meditate? How many people loved you, or prodded you? Told you about their meditation practice? Challenged you so that you decided to look for more inner calm and understanding? What about those who hurt you, brought you to an edge of some kind so that you thought, *I've really got to find another way* or *I've got to look for another level of happiness?* They may be a part of why you're readng these words. We are each swept into the here and now by a confluence of events, causes, and conditions. A large community brought you to this moment.

You can make your sense of that human community even larger. Here are ten ways you can deepen your practice of loving-kindness, not only this week but also in the weeks beyond.

TEN WAYS TO
DEEPEN YOUR PRACTICE

~~~~~

1. **Think of kindness as a strength, not as a weakness.** Kindness isn't an ally of foolishness or gullibility, but rather an ally of wisdom and courage.

2. **Look for the good in yourself**—not as a way to deny your difficulties or problems but as a way to broaden your outlook so it's more truthful and balanced. Looking for the good in ourselves helps us see the good in others.

3. **Remember that everyone wants to be happy.** If we look deeply into any kind of behavior, we will see an urge to feel a part of something greater than our own limited sense of self, a desire to feel at home in this body and mind. This urge toward happiness is often twisted and distorted by ignorance, by not knowing where happiness is actually to be found. Remembering what we share inspires us toward kindness.

4. **Recollect those who have helped or inspired us.** Sometimes even a small act of kindness on someone's part makes an essential difference for us. Cultivating gratitude is a way of honoring these people, and also a way of lifting our spirits and reminding us of the power of good-heartedness.

5. **Practice at least one act of generosity a day.** We all have something to give, large or small. It may be a smile, or an attentive conversation. Perhaps you let a stranger get ahead of you in line, or gave a coworker a small gift, or wrote a late-night note of appreciation. Any act of

generosity—whether material or of the spirit—is a meaningful expression of kindness.

6. **Do lovingkindness meditation.** Each day we can take the time to hold others in our hearts quietly and wish them well. This meditation might include someone who has been helpful or inspiring to us, someone we know who is feeling alone or afraid, someone who is experiencing triumph and joy, or someone we are about to meet with some trepidation. We might, depending on the circumstances of our lives, particularly include children or animals in our thoughts. Taking just ten minutes a day to reflect in this way is a powerful path to transformation.

7. **Listen.** Often we have conversations where we are only partially paying attention; we're thinking about the next email we need to send, or what we forgot to mention to the last person we spoke to. Or we decide we know what the other person is going to say, based on past encounters. Reopening that closed file by listening is a powerful gesture of kindness, one that allows fresh responses and transformed relationships.

8. **Include those who seem left out.** In a conversation with a group of people, there may be those too shy to speak. In a room full of partygoers, there may be some who feel out of place. Be the one who opens the circle.

9. **Refrain from speaking ill of others.** A friend told me about a time he resolved not to talk about any third person; if he had something to say about someone, he would say it directly to that person instead. If you feel tempted

to put someone down, assume knowledge of their bad motives, or generally prove their inferiority, take a breath. Even though we might feel a rush of power in saying those words, we ultimately get no benefit from dividing people and sowing seeds of dissension and dislike. There are ways to talk about wrong behavior without derision or condemnation.

10. **"Walk a mile in another person's shoes before you pass judgment."** As this old saying suggests, even if we're going to take strong action to try to change someone's behavior, a sense of empathy and understanding for them won't weaken us. If anything, that element of kindness will allow us to act more compassionately and creatively.

Keeping the Practice Going

"JUST PUT YOUR BODY THERE"

A FRIEND INVITED ME OUT TO LUNCH one day and offered the following confession: "I've been meditating for about three years now," he said, "and I'd have to say honestly that my experience when I'm sitting in meditation isn't what I thought it would be or should be. I still have ups and downs; my mind wanders and I start over; I still have bouts of sleepiness or restlessness.

"But I'm like a completely different person now. I'm kinder and more patient with my family and friends, and with myself. I'm more involved with my community. I think more about the consequences of my actions, and about what habitual responses I bring to a situation. Is that enough?"

"Yeah," I replied, beaming at him. "I think that's enough!"

This is why we practice meditation—so that we can treat ourselves more compassionately; improve our relationships with friends, family, and community; live lives of greater connection; and, even in the face of challenges, stay in touch with what we really care about so we can act in ways that are consistent with our values.

One of the things I've always found so interesting about meditation practice is that the arena can seem so small—just you in a room—but the life lessons, the realizations and understandings that arise from it, can be pretty big.

The process is one of continually trying to greet our experience, whatever it is, with mindfulness, lovingkindness, and compassion; it helps us realize that everything changes constantly and to be okay with that. The effort we make in meditation is a willingness to be open, to come close to what we have avoided, to be patient with ourselves and others, and to let go of our preconceptions, our projections, and our tendency not to live fully.

Meditation practice helps us relinquish old, painful habits; it challenges our assumptions about whether or not we deserve happiness. (We do, it tells us emphatically.) It also ignites a very potent and alive energy in us. With a strong foundation in how to practice meditation, we can begin to live in a way that enables us to respect ourselves, to be calm rather than anxious, and to offer caring attention to others instead of being held back by notions of separation.

But even when you know that these benefits make meditation well worth the effort, it can be hard to keep up a new meditation practice. In the following pages you'll find some suggestions for strengthening your commitment in the coming weeks.

NUTS AND BOLTS

Try for a daily practice, with sessions at least twenty minutes long. See if you can manage some thirty to forty-five-minute sessions.

Over the past four weeks, you've had the chance to experience a variety of meditation practices. Pursuing any of them would be fruitful. For the next month or so, do primarily one meditation per session. As you gain more experience and confidence, you might divide the session—between, say, a Core Breathing Meditation and a Lovingkindness Meditation, or a Walking Meditation and a Meditation on Emotions. The choice is up to you. The Core Meditation remains our anchor, and a walking or movement meditation is always a good way to bring practice into an activity of daily life. There are times you may want to focus more on the body, so you'll choose an exercise like the Body Scan you learned in Week Two. If you're feeling anxious or unsettled, a Lovingkindness Meditation might be a good choice. What's most important is that you're actually practicing, taking the skills of concentration, mindfulness, and lovingkindness, and making them real.

I used to feel, very early in my practice, that mindfulness was awaiting me somewhere out there; that it was going to take a lot of effort and determination, but somehow, someday, after a great deal of struggle, I was going to claim my moment of mindfulness—sort of like planting a flag at the top of a mountain.

My view of the matter was enlarged and my understanding transformed when I realized that mindfulness wasn't inaccessible or remote; it was always right there with me. The moment I remembered it—the moment I noticed that I was forgetting to practice it—there it was! My mindfulness didn't need to get better, or be as good as somebody else's. It was already perfect. So is yours. But that truth is easily forgotten in the midst of our busy lives and complicated relationships. One reason we practice is to recall that truth, so that we can remember to be mindful more and more often throughout the day, and remember more naturally. Regular practice makes mindfulness a part of us.

Meditation is never one thing; you'll experience moments of peace, moments of sadness, moments of joy, moments of anger, moments of sleepiness. The terrain changes constantly, but we tend to solidify it around the negative: "This painful experience is going to last the rest of my life." The tendency to fixate on the negative is something we can approach mindfully; we can notice it, name it, observe it, test it, and dispel it, using the skills we learn in practice.

As you continue with your meditation practice, each session may be very different from the one that preceded it, just as each has been during this introductory month. Some sittings feel great, and some are painful, with an onslaught of all of the hindrances magnified. But these varied experiences are all part of our process. A difficult session is just as valuable as a pleasant one—maybe more so, because it holds more potential lessons. We can look mindfully at joy, sorrow, or anguish. It doesn't matter what's going on; transformation comes from changing our relationship to what's going on.

I was recently teaching with psychiatrist and author Mark Epstein. He told the class that since beginning his meditation practice in 1974, he'd tried to attend a retreat each year. And from the start he's kept a notebook in which he jots the most compelling insight of the retreat, along with the teacher's single most illuminating, profound, or provocative statement. A few years ago, he told us, he decided to reread his notebook. He was startled to find that year after year, he'd recorded some variation of the same thing: "What arises in our experience is much less important than how we relate to what arises in our experience."

Mark's central discovery can be restated in several ways: "No matter what comes up, we can learn new ways of being with it." "We have a capacity to meet any thought or emotion with mindfulness and balance." "Whatever disagreeable emotion is coursing through us, we can let it go." Rereading those words may keep you going when sitting down to practice is the last thing you want to do.

A saying attributed to Albert Einstein goes, "The problems we face cannot be solved by the same level of thinking that created them." Breaking away from our habitual ways of looking at things, thinking at a new level, and responding differently take a good deal of courage. Here are some ways to help you rally when your courage flags—when you feel too scared (or tired or bored or stiff in the knees) to continue your practice:

START OVER

If your self-discipline or dedication seems to weaken, first of all remember that this is natural and you don't need to berate yourself for it. Seek inspiration in the form that works best for you—reading poetry or prose that inspires you, communicating with like-minded friends, finding a community of meditators, maybe a group to practice with. Or form your own meditation group. If you haven't been keeping a meditation journal (see page 63), start one. And keep in mind that no matter how badly you feel things are going, no matter how long it's been since you last meditated, *you can always begin again.* Nothing is lost; nothing is ruined. We have this very moment in front of us. We can start now.

The meditations in this book are excellent tools for starting over. They're meant to be read and listened to again and again. Don't dismiss them, saying to yourself, *I heard that already, and I get it.* They repay revisiting; they are opportunities to practice, and they deepen over time. Each time you use one of the meditations again, it's different. Work with these meditations daily, and watch how you feel connected one day and drift off the next. The hard day and the easy day each teaches you a lot. And the next day holds the promise of a fresh, new experience.

"JUST PUT YOUR BODY THERE"

I once complained to my teacher Munindra-Ji about being unable to maintain a regular practice. "When I sit at home and meditate and it feels good, I'm exhilarated, and I have faith and I know that it's the most important thing in my life," I said. "But as soon as it feels bad, I stop. I'm disheartened and discouraged so I just give up." He gave me quite a wonderful piece of advice. "Just put your body there," he said. "That's what you have to do. Just put your body there. Your mind will do different things all of the time, but you just put your body there. Because that's the expression of commitment, and the rest will follow from that."

Certainly there's a time to evaluate our practice, to see if it's useful to us and worth continuing. But the evaluation shouldn't happen every five minutes, or we'll be continually pulling ourselves out of the process. And when we do assess our progress, we need to focus on the right criteria: Is my life different? Am I more balanced, more able to go with the flow? Am I kinder? Those are the crucial questions. The rest of the time, just put your body there.

You may think, *I'm too undisciplined to maintain a practice.* But you really can manage to put your body there, day in and day out. We're often very disciplined when it comes to external things like earning a living, getting the kids off to school, doing the laundry—we do it whether we like it or not. Why can't we direct that same discipline (for just a few minutes each day) toward our inner well-being? If you can muster the energy for the laundry, you can muster the energy to "put your body there" for a happier life.

REMEMBER THAT CHANGE TAKES TIME

Meditation is sometimes described this way: Imagine you're trying to split a huge piece of wood with a small ax. You hit that piece of wood ninety-nine times and nothing happens. Then you hit it the hundredth time, and it splits open. You might wonder, after that hundredth whack, *What did I do differently that time? Did I hold the ax differently; did I stand differently? Why did it work the hundredth time and not the other ninety-nine?*

But, of course, we needed all those earlier attempts to weaken the fiber of the wood. It doesn't feel very good when we're only on hit number thirty-four or thirty-five; it seems as if we aren't making any progress at all. But we are, and not only because of the mechanical act of banging on the wood and weakening its fiber. What's really transformative is our willingness to keep going, our openness to possibility, our patience, our effort, our humor, our growing self-knowledge, and the strength that we gain as we keep going. These intangible factors are the most vital to our success. In meditation practice, these elements are growing and deepening even when we're sleepy, restless, bored, or anxious. They're the qualities that move us toward transformation over time. They're what splits open the wood, and the world.

USE ORDINARY MOMENTS

You can access the forces of mindfulness and lovingkindness at any moment, without anyone knowing you're doing it. You don't have to walk excruciatingly slowly down the streets of a major metropolis alarming everyone around you (in fact, please don't); you can be aware in less obvious ways.

Rest your attention on your breath, or feel your feet against the ground—in a meeting, during a telephone conversation, walking the dog; doing so will help you be more aware of and sensitive to all that is happening around you. Throughout the day, take a moment to stop your headlong rush and torrent of doing to simply be—mindfully eating a meal, feeding a baby, or listening to the flow of sounds around you. Even in difficult situations, this pause can bring a sense of connection or relief from obsessing about what you don't have now or about what event or person might make you happy someday in the future.

Once when I was teaching a retreat, I had to go up and down a flight of stairs many times a day. I decided to make walking on that staircase part of my practice. Every time I went up or down I paused first to remind myself to pay attention. It was useful, and it was fun. I've also resolved to do lovingkindness practice whenever I find myself waiting. Waiting on line in the grocery store. Sitting and waiting in a doctor's office. Waiting for my turn to speak at a conference. And I count all forms of transportation as waiting (as in waiting to get to the next place or event)—so on airplanes, subways, buses, in cars, and when walking down the street, I begin: *May I Be Peaceful;*

May I Be Safe; May I Be Happy. Why not, in those "in between" times, generate the force of lovingkindness? You're likely to find that this weaving of meditation into everyday experience is a good way of bringing your meditation practice to life.

MAKE SURE YOUR LIFE
REFLECTS YOUR PRACTICE

Many years ago my colleagues and I at the Insight Meditation Society hosted a teacher from India and accompanied him around the country, introducing him to various communities where interest in meditation was growing. At the end of the tour we asked him what he thought of America. "It is wonderful, of course," he said, "but sometimes students here remind me of people sitting in a rowboat and rowing with great earnestness, but they don't want to untie the boat from the dock.

"It seems to me," he went on, "that some people here want to meditate in order to have great transcendent experiences or amazing alternate states of consciousness. They may not be too interested in how they speak to their children or treat their neighbor."

The way we do anything can reflect the way we do everything. It's useful to see whether our lives outside of meditation practice are congruent with our lives as we sit. Are we living according to our deepest values, seeking the sources of real happiness, applying the skills of mindfulness, concentration, and lovingkindness throughout all areas of our lives? As we practice, that begins to happen naturally over time, but in the meantime we can look at our lives to see if there's any disharmony we want to address. Are there disconnections between our values in meditation and our values in the world—our habits of consumption, for example, or how we treat a particular person, or how well we take care of ourselves? If we find something off-kilter, we have the tools to work for balance.

FAQs

Q How do I know if I'm meditating right? When will I see a change in myself?

A Remember that success in meditation is not based on accumulating wondrous experiences. You aren't in a contest to see how many conscious breaths you can tally up. You are transforming your mind by gently, compassionately beginning again each time you've been lost in thought. You're learning to be with your body, emotions, and thoughts in a different way. Remember that we don't meditate to get better at meditating; we meditate to get better at life.

This transformation may show up as visible changes in your daily life even more than in your formal practice. In fact, others may notice that you're changing before you do. Over time you will see that you can bring more balance and awareness to any experience. One of your most profound and far-reaching transformations will be a growing conviction that you are indeed capable of loving yourself and others.

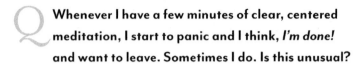

Q Whenever I have a few minutes of clear, centered meditation, I start to panic and I think, *I'm done!* and want to leave. Sometimes I do. Is this unusual?

A Many people describe exactly that feeling. Their scattered energy is getting collected, and they're feeling deep peace or even bliss—and that can be frightening. Even positive states of mind can be alarming if we're unused to them.

There are ways of broadening your field of awareness to incorporate both the fear and the distress. It could be as simple as listening to sounds arising naturally in the environment, which would create more inner space to contain the distress, or getting up and doing a walking meditation, which would generate energy to balance the deep calm that's frightening you. Or you could do a lovingkindness practice, which is also expansive. Whatever action you take, it would be good to stay with the meditation period you've set aside for yourself and not just stop whenever you have the thought *I'm done.* To have the continuity of a set practice is really important. Then you can work with the energy so that it's not a struggle.

Q A daily practice seems so hard. How do I commit to that?

A The best way to make meditation a part of your life and your being is to do a daily practice. But that can be difficult; it can feel like too big a commitment. My colleague Joseph Goldstein once resolved that he wasn't going to go to

202

sleep at night until he'd at least gotten into a sitting posture at some point during the day. That's a thirty-second commitment.

I'd suggest trying that: If you haven't formally practiced during the day, before going to bed, just sit down and assume the posture you usually meditate in. Notice if and how it affects your state of mind. Of course, sometimes getting into the posture tricks us into meditating. The resistance is usually about beginning, and less often about continuing.

If you do fulfill this commitment just before going to bed, notice whether it seems to affect the quality of your sleeping and dreaming. I feel that I sleep better if I meditate just before going to bed because I'm not carrying all the jittering and jangling thoughts of the day with me.

This resolve is not like saying, "I'm going to sit for two hours every day and for half the weekend." It may not even be a five-minute commitment. Even if it turns out to be a thirty-second commitment, at least you went within and had a sense of connecting to yourself.

Q **I've tried meditating a couple of times before, and my resolve lasts about a week. What can I do differently this time so that I stick with it?**

A Sometimes it helps simply to acknowledge the difficulty of keeping a meditation practice going. Difficult, however, does not mean impossible. You might learn a lot by looking at what makes you most readily give up. For me, it was usually self-judgment and impatience, or the feeling that

I had lost something that seemed to glisten just yesterday when my sitting was more peaceful. Eventually I developed a more long-term perspective and could see that my practice sessions were generative and important even when I felt like nothing was happening.

When we opened the Insight Meditation Society in 1976, we received two unusually addressed letters within a month. The first was addressed to the Instant Meditation Society, which made a kind of wonderful sense, given the generally hasty nature of our world. The other was addressed to the Hindsight Meditation Society. That, too, I found revealing—because it's often only in hindsight that we realize that the effort and commitment we put out was worth it.

Something that often helps me is dedicating a practice session to the well-being of someone else, so that in effect I am sitting for both of us. I might choose someone who has helped me out, who is troubled or facing difficulty, or maybe someone in government or on the world-stage. This dedication helps me see my meditation session as an offering for not only myself but for others, and this inspires me to keep on practicing. See page 54 for an example of such a dedication.

Q When you find yourself bored with meditation, how do you cultivate interest?

A Sometimes I think that the best thing is to be bored—because that's interesting. Boredom is one of an array of feelings we're conditioned to avoid. The whole structure of our society, from the moment we're born until the moment we die, seems to be built around the effort to avoid boredom. The instant we feel boredom we have to *do* something, *buy* something—anything to avoid the feeling. So it can be pretty interesting to allow ourselves just to sit and be with boredom and pay attention to it.

And then there are other instances when we look to the roots of our feeling bored and apply an antidote. Sometimes boredom comes when our experience is neutral. That's also part of our conditioning—we depend on intense highs and lows to wake up. Opening up and being present to that space in the middle takes effort. Carefully and intentionally tuning in to ordinary experiences—the breath, a sound—helps us with that.

Boredom can also be a kind of waiting. We think that what's happening isn't good enough, and we're biding our time until something significant happens. The antidote is to notice that and be completely present—for one breath. You don't have to care about more than one breath at a time, but really be there for that one. And then the next one. It all comes together in that way.

Usually we count on the object changing to relieve our boredom, but very often it's not the object that's the problem but the fact that we're only half there. The truth is that if we were fully paying attention, the same old object (the breath, our thoughts and feelings, walking, eating an apple, or washing the dishes) wouldn't be so boring.

Q My meditation practice doesn't seem to be going anywhere, and I'm really suffering. Any suggestions?

A A certain quality of suffering can be a good feedback system, a kind of self-assessment. Often we have made a decision, whether consciously or not, about what our practice should look like, and we disparage or dislike everything other than that ideal. We judge our practice, or we judge ourselves. If we can notice ourselves doing the judging, we've learned something important about ourselves.

When our practice makes us suffer, that feeling can teach us a lot about how we habitually respond to lots of things in our life, not just meditation. My response to my knee pain in practice taught me how often I projected physical or emotional pain into an unchanging future and felt defeated by it. My relationship to anger coming up in my practice taught me how afraid I was of certain feelings, and showed me that by denying them, I was granting them greater power. My difficulty with my wandering mind taught me how self-judgmental I was. And learning how to begin again, to open to whatever was happening, to have compassion for myself instead of criticism, taught me that I could relate to suffering in my life very differently.

We all have cherished hopes about what our meditation practice should look like. But the point is not to achieve some model or ideal but to be aware of all of the different states that we experience. That's a difficult message to believe, and somehow we need to hear it again and again.

FINAL REFLECTIONS

O nce I asked a friend how his life had changed since he began his practice. Without hesitation he said that before, whatever happened in his mind felt as if it were taking place in a small, dark, enclosed theater and that all the action onstage seemed to be very overwhelming and solid. Since he started meditation practice, he said, his awareness of what happened in his mind was more like watching an opera at an open-air theater. It was no longer overwhelming, nor did it feel solid and unchanging.

I knew exactly what he meant. Not long before that conversation, I'd attended my first opera, at an open-air theater in Santa Fe, New Mexico. I could see both the stage and the vast sky. Watching the characters struggling with immensely complicated situations and emotions against the backdrop of that open and spacious sky was a fantastic juxtaposition: However dramatic, even histrionic, the action, however much despair or ecstasy was taking place onstage, it was all in the context of that hugely spacious and allowing sky. The practice of meditation is about having an immensity of vision as vast as the sky. It allows us greater perspective. We might not be able to change the circumstances of our lives, but we can change our relationship to those circumstances.

Meditation allows us to stop looking for happiness in the wrong places. Real, abiding happiness, we discover, isn't the result of getting our needs met temporarily. That often leads to an endless cycle of disappointment and escalating desire: The things we pin our hopes on don't prove to be enough; the bar is continually being raised, and then we're on the lookout for something more.

Conventional happiness—the consolation of momentary distraction—is not only transitory, it can be isolating, shot through with an undercurrent of fear. Even when things are going well, we have the nagging feeling—in the midst of our pleasure—that our well-being is fragile, unstable, in need of protection. And the way we're most likely to protect it is to cut ourselves off from compassionately acknowledging the world's suffering, and our own, because we feel that doing so will undermine or destroy our fragile happiness. But in that state of guarded isolation, we can't experience real joy. Only when we acknowledge all aspects of our life's experience can we be truly happy.

Real happiness depends on what we do with our attention. When we train our attention through meditation, we connect to ourselves, to our own true experience, and then we connect to others. The simple act of being completely attentive and present to another person is an act of love, and it fosters unshakeable well-being. It is happiness that isn't bound to a particular situation, happiness that can withstand change.

Through the regular practice of meditation we discover the real happiness of simplicity, of connection, of presence. We cultivate the ability to disengage from unthinking and habitual struggles. We take delight in integrity, and we feel at home in our bodies, our minds, our lives. We see that we really don't have to look outside of ourselves for a sense of fulfillment. We come closer and closer to living each day in accord with this lovely quotation from Wordsworth: "With an eye made quiet by the power of harmony, and the deep power of joy, we see into the life of things."

I often ask my students, "If you learned that there's a simple, safe activity you could do for twenty minutes a day to help a friend in need, would you do it?" They answer, of course they would, eagerly and without question. Spending that same twenty minutes to help ourselves, however, seems to make us uncomfortable; we worry that it's self-indulgent, ego-centric. But helping ourselves *is* helping our friends. Our own real happiness is the wellspring out of which our ability to give to others flows. As Thich Nhat Hanh once said, "Happiness is available . . . please help yourself."

Resource Guide

SOME PLACES
TO LEARN
INSIGHT MEDITATION

UK, AUSTRALIA AND SOUTH AFRICA

Gaia House,
London, England
www.gaiahouse.co.uk

London Insight Meditation
London, England
www.londoninsight.co.uk

Vipassana Meditation Centre
Herefordshire, England
www.dipa.dhamma.org

Kagyu Samye Ling
Dumfriesshire, Scotland
www.samyeling.org

Blue Mountains Insight Meditation Centre
New South Wales, Australia
www.meditation.asn.au

Buddhist Retreat Centre,
Ixopo, KwaZulu-Natal, South Africa
www.brcixopo.co.za

Institute for Mindfulness South Africa (IMISA),
South Africa
www.mindfulness.org.za

UNITED STATES

Insight Meditation Society
Barre, MA
dharma.org

Cambridge Insight Meditation Center
Cambridge, MA
cimc.info

New York Insight Meditation Center
New York, NY
nyimc.org

Insight Meditation Community of Washington
Washington, DC
imcw.org

Insight Meditation Community of Charlottesville
Charlottesville, VA
imeditation.org

Insight Atlanta Vipassana Meditation Community
Atlanta, GA
insightatlanta.org

Common Ground Meditation Center
Minneapolis, MN
commongroundmeditation.org

Madison Vipassana, Inc.
Madison, WI
madisonmeditation.org

Mid America Dharma,
Kansas City, MO
midamericadharma.org

Insight Meditation Community of Colorado
Denver and Boulder, CO
insightcolorado.org

Santa Fe Vipassana Sangha
Santa Fe, NM
santafevipassana.org

Albuquerque Vipassana Sangha
Albuquerque, NM
abqsangha.org

Spirit Rock
Woodacre, CA
spiritrock.org

San Francisco Insight
San Francisco, CA
sfinsight.org

Insight Meditation Community of Berkeley
Berkeley, CA
insightberkeley.org

InsightLA
Santa Monica, CA
insightla.org

Seattle Insight Meditation Society
Seattle, WA
seattleinsight.org

There are many more retreat centers and community classes all around the world.

PLACES WHERE SHARON SALZBERG TEACHES

~~~~

Kripalu Center for Yoga and Health
Lenox, MA
kripalu.org

Tibet House
New York, NY
tibethouse.org

Community Meditation Center
New York, NY
cmcnewyork.org

The Jewish Community Center in Manhattan
New York, NY
jccmanhattan.org

New York Zen Center for Contemplative Care
New York, NY
zencare.org

Garrison Institute
Garrison, NY
garrisoninstitute.org

The Rubin Museum of Art
New York, NY
rubinmuseum.org

Menla Mountain Retreat & Conference Center
Phoenicia, NY
menla.org

1440 Multiversity
Scotts Valley, CA
1440.org

Check the calendar page at sharonsalzberg.com for Sharon's updated schedule.

SHARON SALZBERG'S
ONLINE OFFERINGS

Sharon offers a variety of online teachings including courses, talks, and more.

Sharon's website
sharonsalzberg.com/store

10% Happier
tenpercent.com

Tricycle Courses
learn.tricycle.org

Insight Timer
insighttimer.com

Happify
happify.com

Be Here Now Network
beherenownetwork.com/sharon

SOME SOURCES
OF MEDITATION SUPPLIES

~~~

Here's a list—by no means exhaustive—of websites selling meditation supplies, including pillows, cushions, chairs, benches, mats, and timers. These recommendations come from friends and students.

Chopa
chopa.com

Samadhi Cushions
samadhicushions.com

Dharma Crafts
dharmacrafts.com

Still Sitting
stillsitting.com

Gaiam
gaiam.com

Sun and Moon Originals
sunandmoonoriginals.com

MatsMatsMats
matsmatsmats.com

Carolina Morning
zafu.net

Sage Meditation
sagemeditation.com

Ziji
ziji.com

NOTES

INTRODUCTION

PAGE 3

Tainya C. Clarke et al., "Use of Yoga, Meditation, and Chiropractors Among U.S. Adults Aged 18 and Over," NCHS Data Brief, no. 325 (Hyattsville, MD: National Center for Health Statistics, 2018), ncbi .nlm.nih.gov/pubmed/30475686.

WHY MEDITATE?

PAGE 24

Quoted in Joan Halifax, *Being with Dying* (Boston: Shambhala, 2009).

THE SCIENCE OF MEDITATION

PAGE 26

Sara Lazar et al., "Meditation Experience Is Associated with Increased Cortical Thickness," *NeuroReport* 16 (November 2005): 1893–97, doi.org/10.1097/01.wnr.000186598.66243.19.

Eileen Luders et al., "The Underlying Anatomical Correlates of Long-term Meditation: Larger Hippocampal and Frontal Volumes of Gray Matter," *NeuroImage* 45 (April 2009):672–78, doi.org/10.1016/j.neuroimage.2008.12.061.

PAGE 27

Quoted in Mark Wheeler, "How to Build a Bigger Brain," UCLA Newsroom, magazine.ucla.edu/depts/quicktakes/build_bigger_brain.

Britta Hölzel et al., "Stress Reduction Correlates with Structural Changes in the Amygdala," *Social Cogn Affect Neurosci* 5, no. 1 (March 2010): 11–17, doi.org/10.1093/scan/nsp034.

PAGE 28

Gaelle Desbordes et al., "Effects of Mindful-Attention and Compassion Meditation Training on Amygdala Response to Emotional Stimuli in an Ordinary, Non-Meditative State," *Front Hum Neurosci* 6, no. 292 (November 2012), doi.org/10.3389/fnhum.2012.00292.

Bonnie J. Horrigan and Richard Davidson, "Meditation and Neuroplasticity: Training Your Brain," *Explore* 1, no. 5 (September 2005): 383, doi.org/10.3758/CABN.7.2.109.

PAGE 29

Sara Lazar, in a personal conversation with the author, August 2010.

Paul Condon et al., "Meditation Increases Compassionate Responses to Suffering," *Psycholl Sci* 24, no. 10 (October 2013): 2125–27, doi.org/10.1177/0956797613485603.

PAGE 30

Kathryn Adair et al., "Present with You: Does Cultivated Mindfulness Predict Greater Social Connection Through Gains in Decentering and Reductions in Negative Emotions?" *Mindfulness* 9, no. 3 (2018): 737–49, doi.org/10.1007/s12671-017-0811-1.

Tammi RA Kral et al., "Mindfulness-Based Stress Reduction-related Changes in Posterior Cingulate Resting Brain Connectivity," *Social, Cogn Affect Neurosci* (July 2019), doi.org/10.1093/scan/nsz050.

PAGE 31

Amishi P. Jha et al., "Mindfulness Training Modifies Subsystems of Attention," *Cogn Affect Behav Neurosci* 7, no. 2 (July 2007):109–19, doi.org/10.3758/CABN.7.2.109.

PAGE 32

Heleen A. Slagter et al., "Mental Training Affects Distribution of Limited Brain Resources," *PLoS Biol* 5, no. 6 (June 2007): e138, doi.org/10.1371/journal.pbio.00501.38.

Richard J. Davidson et al., "Alterations in Brain and Immune Function Produced by Mindfulness Meditation," *Psychosom Med* 65, no. 4 (July–August 2003): 564–70, doi.org/10.1097/01.PSY .0000077505.67574.E3.

PAGE 33

Benedict Carey, "Lotus Therapy," *New York Times,* May 27, 2008, nytimes.com/2008/05/27/health/27iht-27budd.13237896.html.

PAGE 34

Amishi P. Jha et al., "Mindfulness Training as Cognitive Training in High-Demand Cohorts: An Initial Study in Elite Military Servicemembers," *Progress in Brain Research* 244 (November 2018): 323–54, doi.org/10.1016/bs.pbr.2018.10.001.

WEEK ONE: CONCENTRATION

PAGE 39

Alain de Botton, "On Distraction," *City Journal* Spring 2010, city-journal.org/html/distraction-13292.html.

Linda Stone, "Continuous Partial Attention," lindastone.net /qa/continuous-partial-attention.

WEEK TWO: MINDFULNESS AND THE BODY

PAGE 104

Christopher A. Brown and Anthony K. P. Jones, "Meditation Experience Predicts Less Negative Appraisal of Pain: Electrophysiological Evidence for the Involvement of Anticipatory Neural Responses," *Pain* 150, no. 3 (September 2010), doi.org/10.1016/j.pain.2010.04.017.

"Meditation Reduces the Emotional Impact of Pain,"
University of Manchester news release, June 2, 2010,
manchester.ac.uk/discover/news/meditation-reduces
-the-emotional-impact-of-pain/.

WEEK THREE:
MINDFULNESS AND EMOTIONS

PAGE 112

Patricia Leigh Brown, "In the Classroom, a New Focus
on Quieting the Mind," *New York Times,* June 16, 2007,
nytimes.com/2007/06/16/us/16mindful.html.

PAGE 140

Willem Kuyken et al., "Mindfulness-Based Cognitive Therapy to
Prevent Relapse in Recurrent Depression," *J Consult Clin Psychol* 76,
no. 6 (December 2008): 966–78, doi.org/10.1037/a0013786.

John D. Teasdale et al., "Prevention of Relapse/Recurrence in
Major Depression by Mindfulness-Based Cognitive Therapy,"
J Consult Clin Psychol 68, no. 4 (August 2000): 615–23, doi.org
/10.1371/journal.pone.0001897.

WEEK FOUR:
LOVINGKINDNESS

PAGE 186

Antoine Lutz et al., "Regulation of the Neural Circuitry
of Emotion by Compassion Meditation: Effects of Meditative
Expertise, *PloS One* 3, no. 3 (February 2008): e1897,
doi.org/10.1371/journal.pone.0001897.

PERMISSIONS

Excerpt from "Escapist—Never" from *The Poetry of Robert Frost,* edited by Edward Connery Lathem. Copyright © 1969 by Henry Holt and Company. Copyright © 1962 by Robert Frost. Reprinted by arrangement with Henry Holt and Company, LLC.

Excerpt from *Mindsight: The New Science of Personal Transformation* by Daniel J. Siegel, M.D., Bantam, 2010. Reprinted by permission of Random House.

Excerpts from "Keeping quiet" from *Extravagaria* by Pablo Neruda, translated by Alastair Reid. Translation copyright © 1974 by Alastair Reid. Reprinted by permission of Farrar, Straus and Giroux, LLC.

THE AUDIO DOWNLOAD:
GUIDED MEDITATIONS

~~~~

Ten of the meditations in the book are available for download online, so after reading the meditation, you can close your eyes and listen to Sharon Salzberg's voice guide you through the practice. Go to hayhouse.co.uk/download and enter the following Product ID and Download Code:

Product ID: 7390

Download Code: ebook

Several meditations contain an introduction track and the actual meditation track, which is closed by the sound of a gong. But these guided meditations aren't meant just for listening; they're meant to be practiced regularly. Your active participation is important, following along with Sharon's voice as best you can, and doing the breathing, walking, or mindfulness exercises on your own during the pauses.

The audio menu and where to find the meditations in the book:

ABOUT THE AUTHOR

Fabio Filippi

Sharon Salzberg is a pioneer in the field of meditation, a world-renowned teacher, and a *New York Times* bestselling author. She has played a pivotal role bringing meditation and mindfulness into mainstream American culture since 1974. Sharon is co-founder of The Insight Meditation Society in Barre, MA, and has authored ten books. Acclaimed for her down-to-earth and relatable teaching style, Sharon offers a secular, modern approach to Buddhist teachings, making them instantly accessible. Her writing can be found on Medium, NPR's *On Being*, the Maria Shriver blog, and *Huffington Post*. Sharon is also the host of her own podcast, *The Metta Hour*, with more than 100 episodes that feature interviews with the top leaders and voices in the meditation and mindfulness movement.

www.sharonsalzberg.com

HAY HOUSE

Look within

Join the conversation about latest products,
events, exclusive offers and more.

f Hay House

🐦 @HayHouseUK

📷 @hayhouseuk

❤ healyourlife.com

We'd love to hear from you!